The Wicked Stage

Other books by Abe Laufe:

Anatomy of a Hit
Broadway's Greatest Musicals

ABE LAUFE

THE WICKED STAGE

*A history of theater censorship
and harassment in
the United States*

Frederick Ungar Publishing Co.
New York

Copyright © 1978 by Frederick Ungar Publishing Co., Inc.
Printed in the United States of America
Designed by Jacqueline Schuman

Library of Congress Cataloging in Publication Data

Laufe, Abe.
  The wicked stage.

  Bibliography: p.
  Includes index.
    1.   Theater—Censorship—United States—History.
I.   Title.
PN2044.U6L3   792'.0973   77-6973
ISBN 0-8044-2492-6

To the Honorable Florence Perlow Shientag
for her definitive explanation of the law involved in suits
against censorship. She substantiated the fact that attorneys
who defend freedom of expression in dramatic art base
their argument on the freedoms inherent in the First
Amendment to the Constitution of the United States.
Defense of First Amendment rights does not signify approval or disapproval of the dramatic productions involved.

Contents

vii

CONTENTS

Illustrations

Photograph Credits

Key to abbreviated forms used below:
Bettmann—The Bettmann Archive, Inc., New York; *Culver*—Culver Pictures, New York; *Curtis*—Curtis Theatre Collection, University of Pittsburgh Libraries; *Museum N.Y.*—Theatre and Music Collection, Museum of the City of New York; *NYPL*—New York Public Library; *Players*—Walter Hampden-Edwin Booth Theatre Collection and Library at The Players, New York; *Theatre Coll. NYPL*—Theatre Collection, New York Public Library at Lincoln Center, Astor, Lenox, and Tilden Foundations; *Yale*—Yale School of Drama Library

Section One: 30, NYPL; 31, Museum N.Y.; 32, Curtis; 33 top left and bottom, Museum N.Y., top right, Curtis; 34, 35, Museum N.Y.; 36, both Curtis; 37, Museum N.Y.; 38, both Curtis; 39, Museum N.Y.; 40, both Museum N.Y.; 41 top, Curtis, bottom, Yale.

Section Two: 79 left, Players, right, Bettmann, 80, both Yale; 81, Museum N.Y.; 82 Museum N.Y.; 83, both Yale; 84, Museum N.Y., 85 top, Bettmann, bottom, Curtis; 86, 87 Museum N.Y.; 88, Culver; 89, Bettmann; 90, Yale; 91 top, Curtis, bottom, Bettmann; 92, Yale; 93, both Curtis; 94 top, Curtis; 94-95 Theatre Coll. NYPL

Acknowledgments

My thanks to the following people for their cooperation and assistance:

Dr. Ford E. Curtis, who made available all resources of the Curtis Theater Collection of the University of Pittsburgh;

The late Drs. Ralph H. Ware and Harold W. Schoenberger of the University of Pittsburgh, who made available their complete files of clippings and lecture notes on the drama;

Mrs. Jean Blanco, for providing me with pertinent information, reviews, and photographs in the Curtis Theater Collection;

Mr. Stephen Hader, for his assistance in finding pertinent data in the Curtis Theater Collection;

Mr. Julian S. Bach, my literary agent, for his encouragement and direction;

Mr. Alan Hewitt, for his suggestions and corrections of historical data;

Dr. Edmund G. Wilson, for his assistance in providing information about censored musical productions;

Dr. Benjamin Perlow, for his patience in checking the manuscript;

Miss Debbie Jurcevich, for her technical assistance in preparing the final draft of this manuscript.

Special thanks to Miss Hannah E. Bechtel for her invaluable assistance in research and editing.

Preface

This volume presents a concise history of censorship in the United States to show the reasons for censorship, the types of restrictions, the people responsible for censoring, the growth of permissiveness, and the forces that have opposed all types of theatrical censorship. It does not, however, include all bans and restrictions on theatrical entertainments because many of them would be repetitive. On the other hand, since the American theater was largely an outgrowth of the English theater, the author has included some references to the types of English censorship that affected American theatrical entertainment.

From its very beginning, the professional theater in the United States was subject to restrictions. In the eighteenth century, the American censors, notably the Puritans in the New England states, objected not only to the depiction of immorality on stage but also condemned the theater in general. In the nineteenth and twentieth centuries, the American theater, despite occasional skirmishes with vice crusaders, developed greater freedom and, without interference from police, produced many plays banned in England.

English and American writers called the theater the legitimate stage, but the word did not have the same connotation in both countries. In England, the word *legitimate* was synonymous with legal, for the legitimate play and the legitimate theater were both licensed by the Lord Chamberlain. The non-legitimate theater presented musical entertainments that did not require a license. In the United States, the legitimate theater had no legal connotation, for the term generally referred to playhouses presenting dramas or musicals that developed a plot.

The omission of offending words from this volume is not a prudish attempt to keep the book free from obscenity. The inferences are made in the spirit of George Jean Nathan's theory that a well-clad woman can be more provocative than a nude; and that dialogue without vulgarity and profanity can often be funnier than a sketch that sounds as though it were a scribbling of back-yard-fence graffiti. If the reader wants specific words, he may find, after wallowing through scripts and criticisms filled with scatalogical dialogue, that a return to the standard, perhaps even a Victorian, vocabulary is a welcome relief.

The Wicked Stage

1

The American Theater Before 1800

CENSORSHIP in the American theater began shortly after the first colonies were settled, for the Puritans who landed in New England had approved of the British restrictions on the drama and had disapproved of the immorality connected with the English theaters. The New Englanders not only considered stage presentations to be a form of pagan worship but also objected to money spent on building theaters. The Dutch who settled in New York and the Quakers who settled in Pennsylvania were also opposed to any form of entertainment.

The first play written in English and presented in the colonies was probably *Ye Bare and Ye Cubb* by William Darby, performed in Accomac County, Virginia, on August 27, 1665, with Darby, Cornelius Watkinson, and Philip Howard, all amateur actors. The three young men were arrested and tried for acting in a play, but they were acquitted and the informer, Edward Martin, was ordered to pay the costs of the trial.

In the Northern colonies in 1685, several ministers denounced such frivolities as theatrical entertainment, and in 1687, Increase Mather, the American Congregational clergyman, became incensed about rumors of play acting in the colonies, although records do not indicate that any plays were presented in this period.

To prevent any attempts at play production, legislative bodies passed laws banning theatrical entertainment. The Pennsylvania Assembly prohibited "stage plays, masks, and revels" in 1700. By 1711, the Pennsylvania Assembly had passed two additional laws prohibiting shows, but all three laws were repealed by the British government. In 1709, the Governor's Council in New York passed a law forbidding prize fighting as well as play acting, and in 1714, when Samuel Sewall, the American jurist and author who presided at the Salem Witchcraft Trials, heard rumors that a play might be presented in the Council Chambers in Boston, he wrote a letter to the Governor and Council objecting to such a presentation. Little is known of the play or players, nor is there any record that any such performance was given.

Theatrical activity in the South, on the other hand, met with little opposition. An early as 1702 the students at William and Mary College presented a "pastoral colloquy" in Williamsburg for the Governor of Virginia. On July 11, 1716, William Levingstone signed a contract to build a theater, the first in America, in Williamsburg for Charles and Mary Stagg. Evidently the venture was not profitable, for the theater was mortgaged in 1723, and was eventually sold and given to Williamsburg as a town hall in 1745.

In January, 1735, a group of players opened a season of three dramatic presentations in a courtroom in Charles-town, South Carolina. (The name of the city was changed to Charleston in 1783.) A subscription campaign was organized to finance the construction of a theater, and in February, 1736, the second season of plays opened at the New Theater in Dock Street, but theatrical activity in

---

4

Charles-town stopped in 1740 when the New Theater was destroyed by a fire that burned down the major part of the city. A second theater was not built until 1754.

Theatrical activity in the North during this same period was apparently limited to Philadelphia and New York. The first record of any theatrical activity in Philadelphia reflected the influence of the British theater. To avoid any interference from Puritanical Londoners who tried to stop dramatic entertainment, all theaters in the vicinity of London from 1576 to 1616 were built outside the city limits. Similarly, in 1723 when a group of comedians presented the first entertainment in the vicinity of Philadelphia, they avoided any conflict with the Quakers by performing their shows outside the city limits and advertised their location with printed handbills. James Logan, the Mayor of Philadelphia, objected to such entertainment, but he also knew that the English governor, Sir William Keith, approved of it. The following year, the New Booth Theater was built on Society Hill, outside the city limits of Philadelphia, and featured acrobats and comedians. None of these early presentations, however, included dramatic plays. The legitimate drama started earlier in New York. George C. Odell, the authoritative historian, listed *The Recruiting Officer*, presented at the New Theater in December, 1732, as the first dramatic production in that city.

The first attempt to present a play in Boston was made in 1750. Two young men, who may have been professional actors, headed a company of local amateurs and produced Otway's *The Orphan* at the Coffee House in State Street. Even though the city officials were strongly opposed to theatrical fare, the number of curious townspeople who crowded into the Coffee House almost resulted in bedlam. The General Court of Massachusetts lost no time in passing a law that not only banned plays but also imposed a heavy fine of approximately five pounds on any person who allowed his property to be used for shows as well as an equally heavy fine on anyone who was arrested for attending a performance. This law killed any further professional productions in Massachusetts until the British occupied Boston in 1775.

The first professional company of actors in the colonies, headed by Walter Murray and Thomas Kean, met no opposition when it arrived in New York in 1750, the year generally designated as the beginning of the professional theater in America, and applied to Governor Clinton for a permit to present plays. During their first profitable season, Murray and Kean produced six serious plays and two farces.

Lewis Hallam, who managed "The Company of Players from London," the second professional acting group in the colonies, had no problem getting permission for his company to perform in Williamsburg, Virginia, in 1752. The following year, however, when he brought his company to New York, he ran into a series of unexpected difficulties. He could not get a license to present plays; he could not find a suitable theater; he discovered that New Yorkers were no longer enthusiastic about the theater; and he found himself stranded in New York. In July, 1753, he published a plea for help and finally received a permit to give plays. Tickets were not sold at the theater but were available at a printer's shop, a bookstore, and a tavern. In 1754, when he brought his actors to Philadelphia, he met even stronger opposition from the Quakers, but townspeople who wanted to see dramatic entertainment were influential in getting Governor Hamilton's permission for Hallam to produce twenty-four plays. The permit specified that Hallam was to give one benefit performance for the city, produce only plays of high moral standards, and pay enough advance security to cover any possible debts. Before the season had ended, the Governor allowed the company to give six additional performances. Hallam also gave a benefit performance, which netted over one hundred pounds, for the Charity School, later called the University of Pennsylvania, run by the Quakers who, despite their objections to the theater, reluctantly accepted the money.

After the Hallams left Philadelphia, the city had no professional entertainment until 1759.

Lewis Hallam died in 1755 and his company presumably disbanded. By 1758, David Douglass, who had married Mrs. Hallam, reorganized the troupe with Mrs. Douglass as leading lady and Lewis Hallam, Jr., as leading man. Douglass then brought his actors to New York. By unwittingly building a theater on Cruger's Wharf without getting a building permit, he antagonized the city officials who refused to grant him a license to produce plays.

Douglass undoubtedly was aware of the subterfuge British producers had used to reopen theaters that the English censor had closed or refused to license. One producer had hit upon the idea of selling tickets, priced from one to three shillings, for concerts at his theater. Between the two halves of the concert, he presented plays, supposedly free to the patrons. A second producer tried the same scheme by presenting a concert that was followed by a play for which no additional charge was made. A third producer, whose theater had been closed, reopened it, presumably operating on a free admissions policy. Patrons who wanted tickets, however, paid four shillings at a nearby candy shop for an ounce of lozenges and received a complimentary box seat; for two shillings, each patron received one half ounce of peppermints and a ticket for the pit.

Douglass resorted to a variation of this British type of subterfuge. Although he planned to stage standard, classic dramas, he told the New York authorities that he wanted to offer a series of lectures which he called "Dissertations on Subjects, *Moral Instructive and Entertaining.*" The city officials, although skeptical, finally agreed to let him present thirteen performances, but the public's response was poor, and he was not allowed to give any additional performances.

When Douglass went to Philadelphia in 1759, Governor Denny, in spite of opposition from the Quakers, permitted him to build a theater outside the city limits. The Assembly, which did not approve

7

of the theater, passed a law, to become effective in 1760, banning all plays, but when city officials tried to enforce the law, the King of England repealed it.

Douglass next went to Newport, Rhode Island, where he knew the Puritans would be as opposed to theatrical entertainment as the Quakers had been. Although he had no difficulty in renting the Public Room of the King's Arms Tavern, he resorted to the subterfuge of advertising his production of *Othello* as a series of "Moral Dialogues." Encouraged by the public's response, Douglass built a makeshift theater that he opened in September with a benefit performance for the poor and closed in October with another benefit performance. In the summer of 1762, Douglass found stronger opposition to the theater in Providence, Rhode Island, than in Newport. He built a temporary theater, but, in an effort to mislead his opponents, called it a schoolhouse. He produced dramas until the Rhode Island Assembly passed a law, which remained in force until after the Revolutionary War, barring dramatic performances and the further building of theaters.

Growing hostility in the colonies toward the English led to a different type of opposition in the mid-1760s. While David Douglass and his company were touring in Virginia and South Carolina, a group of players, which may have been composed of amateurs, were granted permission to give a performance in New York at the theater on Nassau and Chapel Streets. Since the professional actors who had appeared in New York had come from England, the Sons of Liberty, an anti-English organization, assuming that all the actors came from England, created a disturbance as soon as the play started. Within a short time, a riot broke out involving not only the actors but also the rest of the audience. Several people were injured; one actor was badly beaten; and even the playhouse was partially wrecked.

To counteract this growing resentment against the English, David Douglass changed the name of his troupe to "The Old American Company of Players." When he disbanded his company for the summer of 1774, opposition to the theater as well as to the English actors had increased. In October, the Continental Congress passed a law discouraging all types of theatrical entertainment including outdoor concerts and novelty acts, such as tight rope walkers and equestrian shows. In Salem, Massachusetts, for example, a city that opposed stage shows, audiences had enjoyed performances by John Sharp, an expert horseman from England, who stood on two horses, one foot on each, while the horses raced at full speed. New Yorkers saw an even more spectacular horseman, Jacob Bates, who rode four horses. The act of 1774, however, influenced Douglass and several members of his company to leave for Jamaica where they intended to stay until the American crisis was over.

Even though most of the professional actors had left the Colonies by the outbreak of the war, theatrical activities did not stop. From 1775 to 1777, the occupying British forces gave performances in Boston, New York, and Philadelphia. In the American camps, the theater also flickered in spite of Congressional acts against shows as well as the fact that the American forces had less leisure time and money than the British. In a letter to his sister from Valley Forge, dated May 15, 1778, William Bradford, Jr., wrote that he had seen a performance of *Cato* on May 11, and that if the British did not leave Philadelphia, other plays would follow.

Shortly after the Continental Army reentered Philadelphia in the summer of 1778, the Southwark Theater, the first permanent playhouse built in America, was reopened, but only for a short period. In October, Congress passed a new resolution specifying that anyone holding office in the United States who acted, encouraged, or even attended plays would be dismissed. The following March, the Pennsylvania legislature passed another law banning all shows or entertainments.

In 1782, John Henry, one of the first popular matinee idols in America, who had become a manager for the Douglass company, asked the Philadelphia authorities for permission to lecture at the

Southwark Theater so that he could raise money to pay the rent and taxes which had accumulated on the playhouse, but his request was denied. Two years later, Lewis Hallam, Jr., who had taken over the Douglass Company, asked for a repeal of the antitheater act in Philadelphia, but his request was also denied. Hallam, nevertheless, stayed in Philadelphia and reopened the Southwark to give what he called a series of lectures with speeches honoring the soldiers who had died in the war. Hallam's program, however, also included scenes from standard plays.

In 1785 Hallam found that New Yorkers were still opposed to play acting. Once again he resorted to subterfuge by announcing that he was giving lectures, but in September he produced a full-length drama. Since he had no interference from city officials, he continued producing plays. When he offered to donate a hundred dollars for the benefit of the poor, however, the directors of the Alms House refused to take the money because they did not approve of money earned from theatricals.

By the end of the year, Hallam and John Henry had become partners in forming "The Old American Company." Although their productions were popular, a great many New Yorkers objected to the theater, for, in 1786, approximately seven hundred people signed a petition to stop all plays. Their efforts were futile because more than one thousand four hundred people signed a second petition in favor of letting the plays continue.

Two years later, Hallam and Henry started a new season in Philadelphia, still disguising their plays as "lectures," but in October, they defied the law by offering full-length plays. The Quakers demanded that the Assembly enforce the antitheater law, but a group of prominent Philadelphians had already organized a dramatic association to support the theater. By March, 1789, they were successful in getting the Assembly to repeal the antitheater law. Within one week, Hallam began announcing that the Old American Company was producing plays "by authority." In 1792, the yellow fever plague that struck Philadelphia paralyzed trade and forced all theaters to close. The Quakers, who hoped to link the playhouse with the plague, petitioned the Assembly to pass another antitheater law, but their petition was rejected. The theaters remained closed, nevertheless, until fear of contamination from the disease subsided.

An attempt was made in 1792 to start a theatrical center in Boston. A company of actors, headed by several former members of the Old American Company, solicited subscriptions from Bostonians and raised enough money to build a temporary playhouse in Broad Alley. In order to offset opposition from Puritanical New Englanders, the company called the new playhouse "The New Exhibition Room," which opened in August with the actors appearing in a variety of entertainments. By September, not having run into any difficulties, the company appeared in dramas and continued this policy until December 5, when the sheriff stopped a performance of *The School for Scandal* on charges of violating the antitheater law. Although the audience demanded that the players be allowed to finish the performance, the sheriff closed the theater and arrested Mr. Harper, the comanager, who was released the next day. The venture was not a complete failure, for a great many Bostonians had become interested in the theater and began agitating against the antitheater law until it was repealed in 1793. That same year, a second subscription campaign was launched, and 120 subscribers each paid fifty dollars to build a new permanent theater, which opened in 1794.

Mr. Harper became a more astute manager when he next brought a company of players to Providence, Rhode Island. Although he produced standard dramas, he used the same subterfuge as Hallam and Douglass by calling them "lectures." Moreover, he was permitted to use the Court Room for his theater because he agreed to pay all receipts from every fifth night's performance into the city treasury.

In the late 1790s, the yellow fever epidemic continued to close playhouses. In the fall of 1798, over two thousand people in New York died of the plague, and the theaters were kept dark until December. When the Haymarket Theater in Boston opened in July, 1798, fear of the yellow fever had spread to that city. There were so few people in the audience on the second night that the management canceled the performance and kept the theater closed for the rest of the summer.

A new menace—rowdyism—also plagued the theaters in the 1790s. Shortly after the Federal Street Theater opened in Boston in 1794, the manager was unable to cope with the rowdyism that had developed in audiences. People sitting in the gallery threw apples and even stones at the orchestra pit. To curb these disorders, the trustees of the theater appointed a custodian whose duties were to stop "all kinds of disorder" and to see that people were seated in the proper locations. In New York that same year, the Old American Company presented an opera, *Tammany or The Indian,* but on the opening night of March 24, 1794, the audience, displeased with the production, hissed the music written by James Hewitt. The situation in New York grew steadily worse with gallery rioters insulting audiences and actors as well as the musicians. At the first performance of the 1794–1795 season in New York, a representative of the management talked to the audience and promised to get rid of the rowdyism in the gallery. There is little evidence to indicate that he was successful in curbing the disorders.

2

The Nineteenth Century

Early in the nineteenth century, audiences began acting as censors by protesting or by boycotting the box office. Mr. Wignell, manager of the Chestnut Street Theater in Philadelphia, ran into this problem in 1800 when he hired a dance team, Mr. and Mrs. Byrne. Philadelphians, particularly the women, were shocked by Mrs. Byrne's short skirts and walked out during the performance; many people stopped going to the Chestnut Street Theater; still others wrote letters of indignation to the newspapers. Wignell had further trouble with rowdyism in 1801. He had hired a Mr. Fullerton, an excellent actor from the Theater Royal in Liverpool, but Fullerton, who could not tolerate the hissing in the audience, became unnerved and was driven to commit suicide in 1802.

In 1802, in New York, Washington Irving, using the pen name Jonathan Oldstyle, began writing dramatic criticism for the *New York Morning Chronicle*. In his first column, published in December, 1802, he condemned the unruly gallery crowd in New York, the unclean seats in the pit, the people who ate during the performance, the drippings from candles in the chandeliers, and the rotten apples thrown from the gallery. He also recommended "less noise in the boxes, umbrellas for the pit, less grog in the gallery." Irving's comments were not exaggerated, for William Dunlap, the New York theater manager, had brought constables into the gallery to keep order.

There were, however, several explanations for this rowdyism, not only in New York but also in other cities. Many of the theaters had little or no heat. As a result, people bundled up in warm clothing or else huddled around a small fire. Since the theaters had no ventilating systems, the heat in the summer was unbearable. The seats in the pit were so uncomfortable that people often stood, blocking the view of those sitting behind them. Since seats were not reserved, people had to come early if they wanted choice locations. To add to the confusion, bars in theaters were kept open during the entire performance. The managers also contributed to audience dissatisfaction, for instead of presenting programs that they had advertised, they often canceled, postponed, or substituted plays. In New York, Dunlap had to cope with still another menace—smoking in the theater—a practice that he tried unsuccessfully to stop.

Another form of audience protest, closely allied to rowdyism, was lodged against George Frederick Cooke, a famous English actor who was an alcoholic. Quite often, when he was drunk, he would begin losing his voice and managers were never sure that he would be able to give or finish a performance. When he first appeared in an American production, he explained that he was suffering from a cold. Audiences, however, soon realized that he was drunk and hissed until the curtain was brought down. For several years, he toured in the United States, but the success or failure of his performances depended upon the extent of his drinking. In many cities where stories of his alcoholism, his temper, and his rudeness began to circulate, audiences refused to attend performances.

Edmund Kean, another leading actor in the British theater, was far more successful than Cooke when he first came to the United

States, but before he left, he had incited audiences to riot. Kean's first appearance in Boston in February, 1821, was so phenomenal an attraction that tickets were sold at a premium. Instead of waiting until fall, Kean decided to play a second engagement in Boston in May, although he had been warned that many theatergoers would be away at that time of the year. He opened to a good but not capacity house; attendance dropped the next night; and on the third night, when Kean saw that only about twenty people were in the theater, he refused to give a performance even though he was told that more people had arrived. The Bostonians, incensed by Kean's cancellation of the performance, were determined that he would never act in Boston again.

Stories of Kean's temperamental outburst spread to other cities, where attendance dropped, and Kean returned to England. He became involved in scandals, lost favor with the English, who hissed him, and then made the mistake of returning to America. For his New York opening in November, 1825, the theater was crowded, but the people in the gallery had not come to see his performance. The moment Kean walked on the stage, the mob shouted and booed, drowning out the actors. In spite of the shouting, Kean tried to go on with the play even though he was hit periodically with rotten apples or oranges thrown from the upper tiers until the performance ended in bedlam. The next day Kean published an apology in the papers for his rudeness during his first visit to America and asked the readers to give him another chance to act in this country. The following night, Kean gave another performance, this time without interference.

After several more performances, Kean seemed to be winning back his audiences, but instead of staying in New York, he made the mistake of going back to Boston in December. The theater was crowded opening night, just as it had been in New York, and Kean decided he would make an apology to the audience before the play began. As soon as he came on stage, the gallery mob went into action, shouting and throwing fruit, bottles, cakes, and anything else that was handy. Constables tried to restore order, but the rowdyism increased in intensity until it developed into a full-scale riot among the gallery mob, the constables whom they overpowered, and the men in the pit and the boxes. Kean managed to escape from the theater unharmed, returned to England, and never came back to America.

The influence of the Puritans who had banned theatrical entertainment in Massachusetts was reflected in the 1820s and 1830s, for Boston was unable to develop into a major theatrical city. Bostonians could support one theater, but when a second opened, both playhouses suffered from the competition. Opposition to the theater outside Boston was even stronger. Several actors from Boston who tried to open a theater in Lowell, Massachusetts, in 1833 were promptly arrested for not "pursuing an honorable and lawful profession."

During the 1840s and 1850s, the rowdyism of gallery mobs to express their disapproval of actors or plays cut theater attendance sharply in several cities. In New York, a riot at the Astor Place Opera House made the earlier demonstrations against Kean seem mild. The scandalous riot indirectly involved Edwin Forrest, one of America's best-known actors. When Forrest had gone to London in 1836, several English critics had ridiculed him for trying to compete with such established English stars as William Charles Macready. On Forrest's second trip to London, the audience hissed him during a performance of *Macbeth*. Forrest felt that Macready had been responsible for this rudeness, and, in retaliation, he hissed Macready during a performance in Edinburgh in 1845. In 1849, Macready came to New York and opened in *Macbeth* at the Astor Place Opera House; that same night, Forrest appeared in *Macbeth* at the Broadway Theater. Forrest's friends, however, crowded the Astor Place Opera House and staged a riot by shouting and throwing fruit and eggs at Macready until they stopped the show. A few days later Macready tried to give a second performance at the Astor Place Opera House, but this time the rioting was worse. The militia was brought to the theater to keep order, and Macready managed somehow to finish the play. After the final curtain was brought down, the rioting continued until the militia began firing into the crowd. Thirty-one people were reported killed (the casualties were given as twenty-two in several accounts), and hundreds were reported wounded (some accounts listed the number of injured as thirty-six). Macready, who managed to escape from the theater unharmed, went into hiding until he could book passage to England. Inferences were made suggesting that Forrest had instigated the riot, but no concrete proof was ever given that Forrest had been responsible for the disgraceful incident.

Salt Lake City emerged as a major theatrical center when Brigham Young, the Mormon President, built a playhouse that opened in March, 1862. This unusual theater, which seated approximately one thousand five hundred people, had perfect acoustics; people sitting in the upper third balcony could hear even the slightest whisper on stage. The pit was considered the best part of the house because it rose on a deep slant so that all spectators could see the stage. Every woman in the cast, regardless of how slight her part might be, had her own clean, well-equipped dressing room. Brigham Young, who had his own box as well as a special rocking chair in the center of the pit, wanted his playhouse to cater to the community, and he instituted the system of renting rows of seats to families. He permitted no rowdyism, drinking, or smoking in the theater. In 1865, he established his own rules of censorship after he presented two visiting guest stars, James A. Herne and Lucille Western, in *Oliver Twist*. In one scene, Miss Western, as Nancy Sykes, had pasted a thin slice of raw meat to the side of her face. When James Herne, as Bill Sykes, struck her and then dragged her across the floor and she turned her face to the audience, the raw meat created the illusion of bleeding. Women fainted, and Brigham Young, who objected strenuously to the gruesome scene, announced that he would not permit any more serious plays that offended audiences to be given in his theater. Real life, he said, was filled with tragedy; the theater, therefore, should entertain audiences.

Public disapproval of scanty costumes flared up periodically through the 1800s. In February, 1827, when Madame Francisque Hutin, a French dancer, appeared in New York, indignant women, objecting to her flimsy costume and short ballet skirts, walked out during the performance. In the 1847–1848 season, Palmo's Opera House in New York, which had been having serious financial problems, tried to bolster box office receipts by introducing a daring novelty act, "living pictures" featuring women who posed in tableaux. Although they wore minimal costumes, the illusion of nudity they created brought vigorous protests and city officials promptly intervened, accused the performers of wearing less than the law required, and banned the act.

Cries against nudity on the stage were even more vocal when Adah Isaacs Menken appeared in *Mazeppa* in the 1860s. The illustrated poster for the drama showed a woman, apparently nude, strapped to a horse's back. In one scene, Miss Menken, who was billed as "The Naked Lady," was supposedly strapped to the horse and rode up and down the simulated hills built on stage. The management insisted that Miss Menken's feat was one never done on stage before by a woman, but audiences were less impressed by her bravery than by her brazenness in appearing on stage practically nude. By modern standards, however, Miss Menken was quite decorously costumed in flesh-colored tights. In *Mazeppa*, which was based on Byron's poem, she played two roles—a Tartar girl and Casimir, the Tartar leader. To make her appearance as Casimir seem more realistic, against the wishes of her manager she cut her hair short and shocked not only the manager but also the audiences. Moreover, she never admitted that she wore flesh-colored tights nor did she allow her maid to reveal this information. Miss

Menken was denounced for her audacity, but her performance made *Mazeppa* a popular box office attraction. Many prominent members of New York's social set undoubtedly saw the play, but they never discussed it, at least publicly, nor did they ever admit having seen it.

The protests against Miss Menken's nudity were mild compared to those unleashed against *The Black Crook* in 1866. The original producers, Jarrett and Palmer, had brought a large troupe of dancers and very elaborate scenery from Europe for a ballet, *La Biche au Bois*, which they intended to present at the Academy of Music. When fire completely destroyed the theater, the producers sold their property, scenery, and costumes to William Wheatley, who decided to incorporate the ballet into a melodrama by Charles M. Barras. Wheatley then remodeled the stage at Niblo's Gardens to include moveable platforms, trap doors, and huge sets that could be raised and lowered mechanically. In addition to hiring fifty workmen, Wheatley invested over twenty-five thousand dollars in new machinery, properties, costumes, alterations, and advance salaries. Production costs were estimated to have been between twenty-five and fifty thousand dollars, an exorbitant investment for 1866.

When *The Black Crook* had its world premiere in September, audiences were stunned by the spectacular production which started at 7:45 P.M. and ran until 1:15 A.M., filled with scenes of dazzling opulence, elaborate stage settings, impressive ballets, and beautiful girls in flesh-colored tights. Most of the critics ridiculed the plot, which developed a variation of the Faust legend in its story of a rejuvenated, evil Baron, and combined it with a story of two young lovers threatened by the Baron. Both stories were embellished with dancing fairies and demons. The *New York Tribune* reviewer said, "The scenery is magnificent; the ballet is beautiful; the drama is—rubbish."

As soon as *The Black Crook* opened, newspaper editors and churchmen branded it as wicked. The song lyrics as well as the dancers and their costumes aroused protests. James Gordon Bennett wrote an editorial in the *New York Herald* calling for police to arrest "all engaged in such a violation of public decency." Ministers who preached sermons against the indecency of the production and the scandalous costumes told their congregations that even attending a performance was a sin. One minister said the dances suggested ancient heathen orgies.

The Black Crook, nevertheless, developed into one of the most popular attractions of the century. Most theatergoers disregarded the attempted censorship by the churches and newspapers and overlooked the ridiculous plot because they were impressed by the sheer beauty of the production, such as the magnificent set that included a grotto with a large lake, or the lavish finale that had curtains of mist, gilded chariots, silver clouds, and white angels. The ballet corps of one hundred young, beautiful girls, headed by a fifteen-year-old ballerina, wore striking costumes, even though they were considered daring for the period. The entire production, in fact, was a forerunner of the opulent Ziegfeld and Earl Carroll extravaganzas of the 1920s and 1930s. Audience interest in the production was so keen that a great many women, who wanted to see *The Black Crook* but wanted to avoid the stigma of being recognized at the theater, wore heavy veils to disguise their appearance. When *The Black Crook* closed on January 4, 1868, it had grossed well over a million dollars and had broken all longevity records in New York with a run of 474 consecutive performances. The popularity of the production continued through the last half of the century, for *The Black Crook* was revived at least six times before 1900.

The popularity of *The Black Crook* probably counteracted any opposition to the rise of burlesque when Lydia Thompson and her British Blondes from London opened in New York in 1868. Her production included songs, dances, and jokes integrated into a story based on Greek mythology. The critics were unimpressed by the libretto but were very enthusiastic about Miss Thompson and her blondes. Moreover, there were few, if any, protests lodged against the type of entertainment even though the shapely but Junoesque blondes wore tights because Miss Thompson insisted upon decorum in her production. Indecency, she said, was not caused by an actress wearing tights—it was the manner in which she wore them. Lydia Thompson and her blondes were popular not only in New York but also on tour, especially in Virginia City. Within a short time, other managers were producing similar burlesque revues, which were "family shows," for they were amusing rather than coarse.

These burlesque shows of the 1870s and 1880s were actually an outgrowth of the minstrel shows. The minstrel revues featured an all-male cast, but the burlesques featured pretty girls in the entertainment, which included songs, specialty acts, and burlesques of well-known plays. Moreover, the burlesques of the 1890s provided excellent training for such performers as Fay Templeton, the beautiful Lillian Russell, and the comedy team of Weber and Fields.

The sleazy burlesque shows that overran the theaters on Forty-second Street in New York in the 1920s and 1930s, until Mayor La Guardia banned all such entertainment, were not a deterioration of the nineteenth-century burlesques made popular by Lydia Thompson and her British Blondes. The twentieth-century burlesque revues were, rather, an outgrowth of the honky tonk shows that developed in west coast saloons after the Gold Rush. These raffish entertainments featured dance hall girls who were notorious for their immorality. They not only enticed men to buy drinks but also were available as companions for the men in the boxes that could be closed off by curtains to insure privacy. In some saloons, the dance hall "girls" included female impersonators. As the saloon entertainments increased in popularity, the great burlesque stars of the nineteenth century made it very clear to the public that they had no affiliation with the honky tonks.

Vaudeville shows, which mushroomed across the country in the 1890s and early 1900s, profited from self-censorship. In the late 1850s, vaudeville houses such as the American Theater in New

York, known as The Variety House, presented raffish, vulgar shows for almost exclusively male audiences. When Tony Pastor, a former circus clown, joined the staff at the American Theater, he changed the format of the productions, made the shows suitable for the entire family, and became known as the "father of American vaudeville."

In the 1880s, B. F. Keith and E. F. Albee started a chain of vaudeville houses that developed into the Keith-Orpheum circuit. Mr. Albee, an excellent businessman, had no objections to the raucous pre-Tony Pastor type of entertainment that had kept the old variety shows from catering to family trade. Keith, on the other hand, insisted that shows must not offend patrons and therefore would not permit profanity, vulgarity, or coarse language in his theaters. Keith's sense of decorum and his censoring to make certain that he presented family entertainment, combined with Albee's shrewd management, resulted in a steady growth of their circuit until they were booking acts for approximately four hundred theaters.

James A. Herne's drama *Margaret Fleming*, one of the first American plays to reflect the influence of Ibsen, was also the most controversial drama of 1890 and 1891. The principal character, Philip Fleming, has a devoted wife, Margaret, and a daughter almost one year old. When Margaret learns that Lena, a servant girl, has given birth to Philip's illegitimate son, the emotional upset causes her to go blind. Philip, after making certain that Margaret and their daughter are financially secure, leaves home. In the original version, Margaret refused to forgive Philip, but Herne rewrote the ending several times. In one revision, he had Philip attempt suicide; in another, Philip had a reunion with Margaret that led optimistic audiences to believe that a reconciliation might follow.

Herne first presented the play at Lynn, Massachusetts, for three performances in July, 1890. When he tried to rent a playhouse in New York and Boston, theater owners refused to book *Margaret Fleming* because they considered it too shocking for audiences, particularly since Herne treated Philip sympathetically instead of depicting him as a villain. Herne, therefore, rented Chickering Hall, a small auditorium in Boston, possibly the first little theater in America, where the play ran three weeks. After several prominent American writers, including Hamlin Garland, William Dean Howells, and Mary E. Wilkins Freeman praised *Margaret Fleming* for its realism, Herne reopened the play at Chickering Hall in 1891, and then was able to book it in New York in December, 1891, and in Chicago in 1892. The play failed, for most of the critics, particularly those who disliked dramas that dealt with unpleasantness, wrote poor reviews. Audiences agreed with the critics not only because they disapproved of the drama but also because they objected to the unhappy ending. In spite of constant revisions made as late as 1915, Herne could not convert *Margaret Fleming* into a drama that would please the critics, the audiences, or the theater owners.

3

From 1900 to 1920

THE FIRST PLAY in the twentieth century to be closed by the New York police, Clyde Fitch's adaptation of *Sapho* from the novel by Alphonse Daudet, was produced in February, 1900, starring Olga Nethersole, a tempestuous actress who financed the production. Miss Nethersole had already shocked audiences by her portrayals of unconventional, immoral women in such plays as *Carmen*, in which she kissed her leading man full on the lips. The scene soon became known as "The Nethersole Kiss" or "The Carmen Kiss."

In *Sapho*, Miss Nethersole played Fanny, a courtesan, who lured and then discarded men until she fell in love with virile Jean. The play included three episodes that stunned audiences. The first was a scene in which Fanny virtually begged Jean to seduce her, even offering to shine his shoes if he would let her stay with him. (Weber and Fields, who seldom missed a chance to capitalize on a hit play, added a burlesque of *Sapho*, which they called *Sapolio*, the trade name for a brand of scouring cake, to their production *Whirl-i-gig*, and satirized this episode by having Weber hand Fanny a shoeshine kit.) The second shocking scene in *Sapho* was a masked ball that critics called an orgy. The most objectionable sequence, however, was a torrid love scene followed by Jean's carrying Fanny up a flight of stairs to her bedroom. The curtain was lowered to denote the passage of several hours; when the curtain was raised, the stage lighting indicated that the time was dawn. Jean came out of the bedroom, quickly ran down the stairs, and exited.

The critics almost unanimously denounced the play. In his editorial in the *New York Journal*, William Randolph Hearst, who called *Sapho* an insult to decent women and girls, wrote, "We expect the police to forbid on the stage what they would forbid in streets and low resorts." On March 5, after the twenty-ninth performance, the police, having been besieged by pressure groups, closed the show and arrested Miss Nethersole on the charge of corrupting public morals. Miss Nethersole was released on bail and placed in the custody of her attorney. Miss Nethersole, her leading man, Hamilton Revelle, her personal manager, and the manager of Wallack's Theater where *Sapho* had been playing were given a magistrate's hearing, but her attorney asked for a trial by jury, which was scheduled to begin in April. Before the case reached the courts, leading suffragists, who organized a vigorous crusade against censorship, were joined by such prominent writers as Arthur Brisbane, Samuel Untermeyer, and Harriet Hubbard Ayers. They circulated a petition, which they sent to the Mayor of New York, protesting the arrest. The trial opened in the criminal section of the Supreme Court on April 3. On April 6, the jury acquitted Miss Nethersole of all charges, and the following day, she reopened in *Sapho*. Columnists reported that audiences may have been shocked, but that very few people walked out on the show.

Sapho aroused a different type of public censorship, however, not for Miss Nethersole, but for one of the actors in the cast who was sending his daughter to a socially prominent finishing school. After the trial, the directors of the school notified the actor that his daughter could no longer be enrolled as a student because a group of mothers had seen *Sapho* and therefore did not think that the actor's child would be "a fit companion" for their own daughters.

The controversy over *Sapho* influenced many of the leading producers to reject Fitch's drama *The Climbers* because they considered it too radical for the commercial theater, since the play opened with women returning from a funeral wearing black mourning costumes, including veils, and the final scene ended with a suicide. Moreover, the producers thought audiences might be offended by an effective but bitter satirical scene showing the women in black haggling over prices with two ladies who wanted to buy the imported dresses that the mourners could not wear for a year. Amelia Bingham, who wanted to play the starring role, invested her own money and produced *The Climbers*. Instead of getting protests from audiences, which other producers had anticipated, Miss Bingham won excellent reviews and had a profitable run in the play.

By 1900, women in tights, instead of shocking audiences, were receiving excellent notices from the critics. In their burlesque extravaganza *Whirl-i-gig,* Weber and Fields featured Frankie Bailey, an actress who became noted for her beautiful legs. In *If I Were King*, produced in 1901, Suzanne Sheldon, who played Huguette, the young girl who dies to save François Villon, received rave reviews from the critics for her disguise as a boy because she wore tights that enhanced her shapely legs.

In 1905, when Arnold Daly produced George Bernard Shaw's *Mrs. Warren's Profession* in New York, the drama aroused almost as much controversy as it had in England. When the Lord Chamberlain had banned *Mrs. Warren's Profession* in 1894, Shaw admitted that even if the play had been licensed, no British producer would have staged it. The censor had rejected the play not only because it dealt with prostitution but also because it implied the possibility of two incestuous love affairs. In order to obtain a license for a copyright performance, Shaw expurgated his play by cutting the entire second act, by deleting all references to Mrs. Warren's profession, and by changing her from a brothel keeper to what Shaw called a "female Fagin." After Shaw received his copyright license, theaters, halls, and hotels where the play might have been presented refused to make their facilities available. Almost thirty-three years after it was written, *Mrs. Warren's Profession* was finally given a license for public performances.

In the United States, the drama had first opened in New Haven in 1902 where it received miserable reviews; audience reaction was equally unfavorable. Between the New Haven production and the New York opening in 1905, Arnold Daly was said to have made changes in the script, but the drama infuriated the New York critics, who denounced Shaw and called *Mrs. Warren's Profession* "an insult to decency." One reviewer referred to the play as "refuse in garbage cans." The city officials also were irate and ordered the New York police to stop the show after the first performance and arrest Arnold Daly and Mary Shaw, the leading lady, on a technical charge of disorderly conduct for presenting an immoral drama dealing with prostitution. They were released on bail, but eight months elapsed before they were tried and acquitted.

In England, *Mrs. Warren's Profession* was not licensed until 1925, but in New York, the play reopened in 1907, again with Mary Shaw in the leading role—this time without protest from vice crusaders or interference from censors.

Harrison Grey Fiske produced Maurice Maeterlinck's *Monna Vanna* starring Bertha Kalich in New York on October 23, 1905, the same night Arnold Daly first presented *Mrs. Warren's Profession.* *Monna Vanna* might well have run into trouble with the censors in New York, as it had in England. Although the play had been well received in European countries, in England the Lord Chamberlain had refused to grant it a license because it included an episode in which the heroine, presumably wearing nothing under her coat, went to the tent of a barbaric soldier in an effort to save her people.

A special society was formed in London to perform *Monna Vanna* for its members, but twelve years elapsed before the play was licensed for public performances. For the New York production, Fiske, who wanted to avoid any problems with police officials, modified the scene that had caused the controversy in London. *Monna Vanna*, which was overshadowed by the protests against *Mrs. Warren's Profession*, actually benefited from the conflict, for it opened not only without any notoriety but also without interference. The play, however, failed to please American audiences and closed after a short run.

Public reaction to Oscar Wilde's short play *Salomé*, as well as to the operatic version with music by Richard Strauss, demonstrated the differences between English and American censorship. In London, the Lord Chamberlain had refused to license Wilde's drama—even though the noted international star Sarah Bernhardt had planned to appear in it—because the play violated the censor's code, which did not permit characters from the Scriptures to be represented on stage. In the 1920s, the censor still refused to license the play because it dealt, in part, with Herod's incestuous desire for his stepdaughter. *Salomé* was finally licensed in 1931. The operatic version, on the other hand, met with little or no opposition in England. In 1910, Thomas Beecham made a special appeal to the prime minister for permission to produce Strauss's opera with Wilde's play as the libretto. To avoid any objections from the censor, the scene showing John the Baptist's head on a platter was deleted, and John the Baptist was called The Prophet. Some time later Beecham revealed that apparently no one in the audience had realized that the cast had sung the original unlicensed text. The Lord Chamberlain, in fact, according to Beecham, had congratulated him on the success of his production.

In the United States, reactions to Wilde's *Salomé* and to the opera were the exact opposite of those in England. The shortness of the play made it unsuitable for the American commercial theater, and, therefore, there were few, if any, comments made about the drama. The reaction to the opera, however, was vehement. *Salomé* had its American premiere on January 22, 1907, with Olive Fremstad singing the title role. Objections to the plot and to the much-publicized Dance of the Seven Veils (performed by Mlle. Bianca Froelich) were so heated that the board of directors refused to allow a second performance at the Metropolitan Opera House. Two years later, Oscar Hammerstein produced it at his Manhattan Opera House in New York. It was then performed very successfully in other cities, and, sometime later, the board of directors at the Metropolitan Opera House reversed the earlier decision and permitted *Salomé* to become part of its repertoire.

The Easiest Way by Eugene Walter might have run into strong opposition from censors because it dealt with immorality. David Belasco, however, who produced the drama in 1909, added several touches that made *The Easiest Way* thought provoking rather than offensive to most audiences. The principal character, Laura Murdoch, the mistress of Willard Brockton, a wealthy Wall Street broker, falls in love with poor but handsome John Madison, who promises to marry her when he is financially secure if she will give up her lover. Laura agrees and tries to earn an honest living, but she is unhappy living in poverty. Brockton offers to take her back if she will tell Madison the truth. She does not, and when Madison and Brockton learn of her deception, they both leave her. As the play ends, Laura is contemplating suicide. Suddenly she changes her mind and tells her maid she is going to Rector's, a well-known restaurant, to have a good time, obviously implying that she hopes to meet a new lover.

David Belasco agreed to produce *The Easiest Way* even though Eugene Walter refused to make any changes in the script. Belasco, on the other hand, refused to use the actress whom Walter wanted to play the lead. Her portrayal, Belasco felt, would have made Laura a jaded, somewhat hardened, ex-chorus girl. Instead, Belasco

Theatre, Water Street.

MONDAY Evening, March 11, 1799.
And Every Evening this Week.
At Mr. G R A N T's, No. 242, Water Street,

Between Beekman and Pecks Slip

Will be prefented a GRAND MEDLEY of ENTERTAINMENTS in 5 Parts,

P A R T I.

Comic Scene between the Old Beggarman & the Termagant Landlady

P A R T II.

By the much admired

Ombres Chinoifes,

Willl be prefented the

BROKEN BRIDGE,

Or the Difappointed Traveller. With the Downfall of

The Impertinent Carpenter

P A R T III.

The ingenious fcene of the SPORTSMAN and his faithful DOG,
Which has never failed of giving univerfal fatisfaction.

P A R IV.

A Grand Collection of Wax-Work Figures, reprefenting the ancient Court of

Alexander the Great,

Their graceful movements have never failed of giving univerfal fatisfaction.
The Performer has fpared neither pains nor expence in the richnefs of their
drefs.

By the curious Pruffian Fantitina will be performed the following Figures:
The Merry Humours of Old JONATHAN and his WIFE,
*A Figure in the character of a Country Girl, will dance a JIG, as
natural as Life,*

A Hornpipe by a fmall Figure in the character of an American Tar.
The aftonifhing Lapland Lady will dance a Jig, and change her Face
three times imperceptible. Likewife a brilliant Collection of FIGURES

Being the richeft of the Kind ever exhibited

A Curious ITALIAN SCARAMOUCH will dance a Fandango,
and put himfelf into twenty different fhapes, being one of the greateft
Curofities ever prefented to an American audience.

Playbill of a performance at New York's Water Street Theater, 1799
(left). Theatrical companies faced many obstacles in that city, including
an epidemic of yellow fever that closed the playhouse for a time in the
late 1790s. Above, the famous Astor Place Opera House in New York
City, where demonstrators staged a riot against British actor William
Charles Macready. The militia had to be called in to keep order and was
forced to fire into the unruly crowd.

Notable actors of the nineteenth century—British actors Edmund Kean (far left) as Richard III and (top left) as Hamlet, and William Charles Macready (top right) as Henry IV. Kean's temperamental outbursts turned audiences against him in the United States, and Macready's New York appearance set off riotous protests by friends of American actor Edwin Forrest, shown left as Richard III. London critics had ridiculed Forrest's talents when he appeared there.

Adah Isaacs Menken (left) in *Mazeppa*. She scandalized 1860s audiences, particularly the women, by cutting her hair short for the role. She also shocked by appearing to be nude while strapped to the back of a horse, as shown above in this illustration for a poster. During the scene the horse galloped over the simulated hills on stage.

When *The Black Crook* opened in New York in 1866, church sermons and newspaper editorials denounced it as wicked. They objected to the song lyrics and choreography, but especially to the scanty costumes.

Two leading actresses at the turn of the century. Olga Nethersole (left) added to her tempestuous reputation by appearing in Clyde Fitch's *Sapho*, which featured a torrid love scene with Hamilton Revelle ending with the heroine's being carried upstairs to her bedroom (facing page). Mary Shaw (right) opened in 1905 in Bernard Shaw's *Mrs. Warren's Profession* and shocked the New York drama critics. Both actresses were arrested for appearing in immoral productions but were later cleared of all charges.

The Easiest Way by Eugene Walter, a David Belasco production, offered what the mixed reviews called "an evening of good acting and bad morals." It was banned in Boston and had censorship troubles elsewhere. Left, Frances Starr as Laura Murdoch, who earns a meager living after giving up her wealthy lover for a poor but handsome suitor. Below left, Frances Starr, Robert Kelly, and Joseph Kilgour, the three principals in *The Easiest Way*.

Richard Bennett, below, and Wilton Lackaye in *Damaged Goods*. This drama of a young man whose physician informs him he has a venereal disease was rejected by all producers. As the playbill shows, its first performances had to be given privately for members of the *Medical Review of Reviews*.

selected young, attractive Frances Starr to portray the amoral but frail and bewildered heroine who must choose between her desire for luxury and her love for handsome John Madison. Although Walter objected to the casting, he still wanted Belasco to produce the drama even though Belasco barred him from attending any rehearsals. To build up sympathy for Laura, and to make certain that she was not depicted as a callous, kept woman, Belasco created the image of a helpless, rather innocent girl by using numerous dolls and toy animals to decorate the set, particularly in the scene in Laura's bedroom.

The play opened to mixed reviews, but most of the critics praised Frances Starr for her portrayal of the unfortunate Laura. Moreover, they were impressed by the fact that the play did not resort to a superimposed happy ending. Charles Darnton in the *Evening World* summarized the opinions of most of the critics with his comment, "An evening of good acting and bad morals."

The Easiest Way stimulated controversial discussions, which aroused audience interest and gave the play a popular run in New York and on the road. In New York, there was no interference from city officials, but on tour, the play did run into censorship problems. *The Easiest Way* was banned in Boston. In Norfolk, the authorities insisted that an episode involving a kiss be cut.

Indirectly, however, the play caused a different type of public censorship in New York, as a result of the final scene in which Laura said she was going to Rector's. The implication that Rector's might be a rendezvous where prostitutes could meet new lovers ruined not only the famous restaurant but also Rector's Hotel, which was forced to close within the next five years.

Clyde Fitch shocked theatergoers with *The City*, produced in 1909, even more than he had in *Sapho*, for he created a drama dealing with incest and blackmail. The drama showed the disintegration of a family that had come from a small town to live in the city. When George Rand, Jr., learns that his father had an illegitimate son, Hannock, a drug addict, who had been blackmailing him,

George conceals this information because he wants to run for governor. George then discovers that Cecily, his younger sister, has married Hannock, and he tells her that Hannock is her brother. Hannock goes insane, shoots and kills Cecily, and then tries to kill himself, but George stops him and turns him over to the police. In the last act, George declines the nomination for governor.

Although profanity had not been permitted on the stage up to this time, Fitch set a precedent by including an oath in the dialogue. At the climax, Hannock electrified the audience by shouting, "You're a goddam liar." The oath was banned in Boston during the tryout, but it was used without interference from the police in New York. Fitch died in September, 1909, before the play went into rehearsal. At the opening performance in December, 1909, according to reporters, when Hannock shouted his oath, several people, including one of the New York drama critics, fainted. When the final curtain came down, the first-night audience gave *The City* a tumultuous ovation. Despite the controversial plot, *The City* drew well for 190 performances. On the road, however, the oath as well as the sordid story offended many people. In Georgia, for example, an infuriated member of a church board and his family walked out on the play.

The Irish Players from the Abbey Theater in Dublin made their first visit to America in 1911 in a season of repertory. All of their productions, with the exception of John Millington Synge's *The Playboy of the Western World*, were well received. When the Abbey Players started their American tour in Boston in October with *The Playboy of the Western World*, members of Irish societies, protesting that the play was an insult to Irishmen, created minor disturbances. This reaction was almost a repetition of what had happened in Dublin when the drama was first produced, for Irish partisans kept interrupting the performance by booing and blowing horns to drown out the actors. Much stronger opposition flared up at the New York premiere in November. No sooner had the curtain gone up than the gallery mob began booing and throwing vegetables until the actors rushed off the stage. People in the gallery continued to shout, demanding that the play be stopped; people in the orchestra threatened to manhandle the actors. The bewildered stage manager tried to start the play, but the gallery mob began hurling capsules filled with asafetida at the stage. As these broke open, the odor in the theater became unbearable. By this time, the police had arrived and tried to restore order by throwing the rioters out of the theater. Even when more police were rushed into action, they could not stop the rioting or the shouting. By the end of the performance, the police had thrown out a great many people but had arrested only ten.

Rioting also broke up performances of the drama in other cities. For a while, a story circulated that the management in several cities had hired hoodlums to create disturbances in order to get newspaper coverage, but the rumor was never verified. Opposition to the play gradually subsided, and *The Playboy of the Western World* was later performed in the United States to appreciative audiences. When the play was revived in 1946, for example, both the New York critics and audiences regarded it as an excellent Irish folk comedy.

Pressure from crusading groups agitating for censorship affected two plays produced in 1913. *Damaged Goods (Les Avariés)* by Eugene Brieux, written in 1902, dealt with hereditary syphilis. A young man, afflicted by the venereal disease, marries against the advice of his physician. When the doctor finds that the young man's child is afflicted by the disease, he refuses to allow a servant to nurse the child because she and her children might also become contaminated. The wife threatens to sue for divorce, but the doctor advises her father against taking such action. The doctor explains that the disease is spread through ignorance and tells the father to advocate legislation that would require anyone who plans to marry to obtain a medical certificate.

In England, the Lord Chamberlain had banned the play; in the United States, *Damaged Goods* had been rejected by almost every major producer on Broadway. Richard Bennett and Wilton Lackaye headed a group that produced the drama, staged by Edward L. Bernays, coeditor of *The Medical Review of Reviews*, for one matinee performance on March 14. Although the clergy strongly protested against the drama, it was performed at a second matinee on March 17. Bernays, who believed that the play should be allowed to continue, solicited subscriptions for *The Medical Review of Reviews* Sociological Fund and received financial support from several prominent citizens. He then followed a practice established in England by organizing the subscribers into a club theater that presented the play for members only. Physicians and scientists endorsed *Damaged Goods* as a clinical study, and in April, the producers were permitted to present the drama on a regular schedule open to the general public.

The favorable reception of *Damaged Goods* in New York as a clinical study did not change the negative reaction to the drama in England. When two Americans, Mr. and Mrs. George Baxter, staged the play in London in 1914, several newspaper editors would not allow their critics to review the production. It was not until World War I that the attitude of the English public changed. Medical reports showed that many soldiers had been crippled by venereal disease, and before the war ended, *Damaged Goods* was considered to be a vital, educational drama that was sent on tour to British military installations to be performed for the troops.

Damaged Goods did not stir up as much controversy in New York in 1913 as *The Lure*, a drama by George Scarborough dealing with a young girl who is almost enticed into working in a brothel. Scarborough, a newspaper reporter and federal Secret Service agent, had based his play on a white slave case he had investigated. Newspaper critics condemned the drama; the *New York Herald* critic said it dealt with problems "not often discussed on the stage or mentioned in polite society." City officials who checked on the show branded it as lewd and immoral and ordered the police to close *The Lure*. Since the Shuberts had produced the play, Lee Shubert, acting as spokesman for the family, testified that *The Lure* was basically a moral drama, and asked that his attorney, Samuel Untermeyer, be allowed to see the play. The judge refused to let the play reopen, but he ordered a special private performance to be given for the grand jury and the attorneys. Lee Shubert, who realized that the court could take action against the Shuberts and close the play permanently, suggested that several scenes could be rewritten. The grand jury agreed to the revisions, and the case was dropped. The revised production later reopened, drew curiosity seekers because of its notoriety, but closed after a moderate run.

Reformers were growing apprehensive about the abbreviated costumes worn in musical revues in the 1910s. Even though audiences had already grown accustomed to seeing women in flesh-colored tights, they were startled when Ziegfeld featured Ann Pennington in *The Ziegfeld Follies of 1913* burlesquing "September Morn," the famous painting of a nude standing in water. Ziegfeld signed Annette Kellerman, who had shocked the public with her famous one-piece bathing suit, to appear in *The Ziegfeld Follies of 1914* in a production number, "Neptune's Daughter," but the sequence was dropped from the show. Kay Laurel, one of Ziegfeld's new, beautiful showgirls, however, wore a flesh-colored version of Miss Kellerman's swimsuit that dazzled critics and news reporters. Photographs of her wearing the swimsuit soon appeared in numerous newspapers and made her one of the first famous, scantily clad pin-up girls in the *Follies*.

During the war years, many of the revues featured patriotic spectacles. Ziegfeld's press agents had no difficulty publicizing one of the patriotic scenes in *The Follies of 1917* with a photograph of Kay Laurel, posing in front of crossed American and French flags and wearing a blouse, wide open, exposing one of her breasts, the picture indicating that the blouse had been ripped by the lustful enemy. The first-act finale in *The Ziegfeld Follies of 1918*, a tableau "Forward Allies" staged by Ben Ali Haggan, included Red Cross workers and French and American soldiers throwing grenades at the invading Germans. The *Follies* girls, fully clad and holding flags of the Allied nations, surrounded Kay Laurel, her bosom exposed, representing the Spirit of France. For this same *Follies*, Alfred Cheney Johnston photographed the *Follies* girls in seminude poses; they wore only a wisp of chiffon, a string of pearls, or a shawl. Ziegfeld used these striking photographs not only for publicity, which emphasized the classic rather than the erotic beauty of the *Follies*, but also as cover designs for the sheet music. During this same period, the Shuberts, who tried to compete with *The Ziegfeld Follies* by producing *The Passing Shows*, made an effort to outdo Ziegfeld by using a runway that brought the ladies of the ensemble, often wearing diaphanous costumes, closer to the audience. Those agitating against eroticism in the theater, however, did not take any definite action about censoring minimal costumes until the 1920s.

4

The Scandalous
Early 1920s

DURING THE 1920s, the United States had no official censor similar to the Lord Chamberlain in England, but it did have pressure groups, self-appointed vigilantes, vice crusaders, and drama critics who protested against permissiveness in the theater. In the early 1920s a group of license commissioners, police commissioners, and directors of public safety began discussing means of stopping the increased number of peep shows spreading throughout the country. By 1921, bare legs on stage had been banned in New York, and orders were issued to subdue suggestive dances in musical revues. The American drama critic, George Jean Nathan, alarmed by these discussions of restrictions, compared the actions of city officials to the edicts of the Lord Chamberlain in England. Yet during this same period, *The Ziegfeld Follies of 1922* featured Gilda Gray, the torrid shimmy dancer. In *The Mimic World*, Mae West did the shimmy sitting down. "The Maid of Gold," a production number in *The Ziegfeld*

Follies of 1924 featured Muriel Stryker, an exotic dancer, her body painted with gilt.

Agitators for censorship objected to a bawdy French farce, *The Demi-Virgin*, adapted by Avery Hopwood and produced in 1921. The flimsy plot dealt with two motion picture stars who are married, separated on their wedding night, and finally reunited. The editors of the *New York Times*, who also objected to the play because it included a strip poker scene, refused to print any advertisement that included the title of the show. This attempt at censorship backfired, however, for Al Woods, the producer, instead of protesting against the ban, inserted a daily advertisement in the *Times* citing the number of people who had seen a popular play at the Eltinge Theater but did not mention the name of the play or the author. Woods's gimmick advertisement brought excellent results, for *The Demi-Virgin* drew crowds of curiosity seekers and outran many of the spicier farces Woods had produced.

Reformers who had been crusading for censorship of the theater were ready to move into an active campaign when *The God of Vengeance* by Sholem Asch opened in December, 1922, at the Provincetown Theater in Greenwich Village. Rudolph Schildkraut starred as Yekel, the owner of a brothel in Poland, who has married one of the prostitutes in the house. His eighteen-year-old daughter does not know about his establishment or her mother's past, but the madam of the house maneuvers to get the girl to the brothel, and as the play ends, Yekel is cursing his wife and child. Despite pressure from reformers who were registering strong protests for censorship, *The God of Vengeance* ran 133 performances before the police were ordered to close the show. The case was tried in court, and the jury voted against the producer and the principal actors who were convicted for presenting an immoral drama. This court action helped temporarily to calm the increasing number of vice protestors.

A number of Broadway producers were amazed that Luigi

Pirandello's *Six Characters in Search of an Author* opened in New York in 1922 without opposition, protests, or comments on the reference to incest that had caused the British censor to ban the play. New Yorkers, in fact, responded more favorably to the drama than the critics who objected to the obscurity of the plot.

The crusaders for reform in the theater became incensed in 1923 over the extent of nudity in musical revues. Production numbers in *The Passing Show of 1923* featured nude figures on chandeliers, as tassles on a living curtain, and as ingredients in a large fruit basket. In his first revue, *Vanities of 1923*, Earl Carroll featured nudes in living curtains, very similar to scenes in the French revue *Folies Bergère. Artists and Models* went even further, for the nude or seminude showgirls moved about on stage. Up to this time, nude figures had been permitted only if they were immobile. The reformers intensified their protests until city officials promised to take action. Since the greatest number of complaints had been lodged against the *Vanities* and its minimal costumes, which consisted of a G-string and perhaps a few well-placed beads, the police were ordered to make periodic checks on Carroll's production. Stories about a show being investigated made excellent news copy and bolstered ticket sales. No drastic action was taken in New York, but in Philadelphia, the mayor closed the Shubert production *Ted Lewis's Frolic*, calling it "salacious" and "offensive." The Shuberts went to court and obtained an injunction that prevented the mayor from closing the show; the mayor retaliated by revoking the license for the Shubert Theater. Once again the Shuberts went to court, won the case, and reopened the theater with *Ted Lewis's Frolic*.

A different type of censorship developed in 1924 in connection with *What Price Glory?* by Maxwell Anderson and Laurence Stallings, one of the first American plays to depict the brutality and futility of World War I. Captain Flagg and Sergeant Quirt, the two principal characters, hate each other as men, respect each other as soldiers, and compete for the conquest of a French tavern owner's daughter, Charmaine, who has affairs with both of them. They do not think of war as a glorious adventure, and they rebel against senseless orders that can lead only to certain death for the men. Yet in the final scene, Flagg, who is drunk, and Quirt, who is wounded, are ready to go back into the fight. Most of the critics called *What Price Glory?* a significant drama, but several reviewers thought the dialogue, although realistic for soldiers in combat, too earthy for the stage. Cries for censorship arose, but city officials did not ask for revisions or cuts.

The Pulitzer Prize Committee, however, became involved in arguments over the merits of the drama in the spring of 1925. Two of the jurors, Jesse Lynch Williams and Clayton Hamilton, named *What Price Glory?* as their selection for the Pulitzer Prize, but Hamlin Garland, the senior member of the committee, objected to the frank dialogue and refused to recommend the Anderson-Stallings drama. Williams and Hamilton finally agreed to support Garland's recommendation and awarded the prize to Sidney Howard's *They Knew What They Wanted.* Champions of the Anderson-Stallings drama censured the Pulitzer Board for its indirect censorship in bypassing *What Price Glory?*, but they also admitted that Sidney Howard had written an excellent drama in his modernization of the Tristram legend. The story, set in the Napa Valley, dealt with an older man whose young wife is seduced by a youthful lover. Sidney Howard also used realistic language and profanity in the dialogue of the vineyard workers, but critics found it less offensive than the dialogue in the Anderson-Stallings drama.

Both *What Price Glory?* and *They Knew What They Wanted* were mild in comparison with the gamier plays that the vice crusaders denounced in 1924 and 1925. The district attorney's office was deluged with demands for censorship of the immorality, licentiousness, and frank dialogue in the theater; but his office was also besieged with protests from civil liberty organizations and Actors Equity, which opposed the principle of censorship or restriction. After an appeal from the district attorney to producers to tone down their productions brought no tangible results, the district attorney and the protest committees agreed on a compromise proposal. A jury, selected from representative actors and representatives from churches and protest committees, would be organized to investigate the more controversial or offensive dramas. These jurors, who were to attend the plays individually rather than in groups, would report to the district attorney. He would then decide what action should be taken.

Plays that had caused the movement for censorship to gain momentum included *Simon Called Peter* by Jules Eckert Goodman and Edward Knoblock, produced in 1924. The story of a priest who is tempted by two women and leaves the church to marry a nurse scandalized reformers, especially during the scene in which one of the women opened her blouse to entice the hero. The play might have been a quick failure if publicity about the shocked crusaders had not interested enough curiosity seekers to keep the play running eighty performances. *Simon Called Peter*, however, closed before the investigating jurors went into action.

In December, 1924, David Belasco produced *The Harem*, adapted by Avery Hopwood from a comedy by Ernest Vajda. The play was banned in London but was presented in a private club theater. In the Belasco production, Lenore Ulric starred as Carla, who disguises herself as a sultan's favorite and seduces her own husband. Although the protestors agreed that *The Harem* bordered on the salacious because it emphasized sex, they decided not to include it in their list of dramas to be investigated.

William A. Brady announced that since other producers were making money presenting immoral plays, he would stage a drama that would force a showdown on the problem of censorship. In February, 1925, he produced *A Good Bad Woman* by William J. McNally, the story of a streetwalker who comes back to her home town, gets a position taking care of a wealthy woman, seduces a young man, gets another into a compromising situation, and finally involves her father in a murder. The play, which ran only sixteen performances, closed before the list of plays to be checked was completed, but it triggered the district attorney's office into selecting jurors to investigate several plays including *They Knew What They Wanted, The Firebrand, Ladies of the Evening,* and *Desire Under the Elms.*

The *New York Times* interviewed several of the jurors, including a professor of English at Columbia University, the editor of *Scribner's* magazine, a woman active in civic affairs, an economist, the wife of a novelist, an architect, a writer, and a musician. In making the survey, the *Times* reporter learned that the jurors were asked to answer two questions: Are any portions of the play under consideration objectionable from the point of view of public morals? Is the play as a whole objectionable from the point of view of public morals? The *Times* reported that most of the committee members agreed that their fellow jurors were reasonable and intelligent, and that all of them had often based their judgment on taste rather than morals.

Several of the jurors did not object to *They Knew What They Wanted.* Their final decision was in favor of leaving the play unchanged. Moreover, they said they would encourage people to see it because Sidney Howard had written a drama of merit.

Critics called *The Firebrand* by Edwin Justus Mayer amusing and satirical but adult entertainment. The play developed the romance of Cellini, played by Joseph Schildkraut, and the beautiful Angelica, whose mother had sold her to him. Involvements with a duke and duchess almost lead to Cellini's death, but the duchess clears him of all charges. Cellini, knowing that Angelica can bring him nothing but trouble, gives his young mistress to the duke and then furtively arranges for a rendezvous with the duchess. When the committee discussed the drama, one juror recommended that Joseph Schildkraut's performance as Cellini be toned down; most of the jurors thought that a scene on a balcony could be shortened without changing the quality of the drama. One of the play's producers, who came to the discussion, agreed with the jurors and, at the request of the district attorney, agreed to make the changes suggested by the committee. The producers complied with the district attorney's request, and *The Firebrand* continued its profitable run.

Ladies of the Evening by Milton Herbert Gropper, produced by David Belasco, was a variation of *Pygmalion* in its story of an artist who makes a bet that he can pick up a streetwalker and change her into a respectable woman within a year. The investigators made only one recommendation—that a scene be changed from a bedroom to a street corner. In response to an order from the district attorney's office, the script was revised and the play had no further interference from the investigators.

The greatest controversy arose over Eugene O'Neill's *Desire Under the Elms*, which the Provincetown Players produced off Broadway at the Greenwich Village Theater with Walter Huston, Charles Ellis, and Mary Morris heading the cast. A. L. Jones and Morris Green bought an interest in the drama and then moved it uptown to a Broadway theater. When word spread that the play was to be investigated by the district attorney's office, box office receipts jumped more than five thousand dollars in one week. The people who crowded the theater were curiosity seekers, who came to see a lewd show, rather than regular drama patrons. At one performance, the audience was so noisy that one of the principal actors stopped the play and said it would not continue until the audience quieted down. Opinions on the merits of *Desire Under the Elms* differed. Some objectors thought the drama presented distorted characterizations of New Englanders. Many of the critics, however, praised the drama as a realistic tragedy and were very much impressed with the unusual stage set showing four rooms in the house as well as the outside of the house, thus making it possible to have simultaneous action in two or three different rooms.

The story involved Ephraim Cabot, aged seventy-five, who has married for the third time; Abbie, his young wife; and Eben, his youngest son. Abbie and Eben have an affair, and when their child is born, Ephraim thinks he is the father. To prove that she loves Eben, Abbie murders the child, who would have inherited the farm. The district attorney in New York, Joab H. Banton, ordered the play closed, but this action immediately incited strong protests from critics, dramatists, actors, and other members of the community. A group of writers, including William Allen White, Percy MacKaye, Don Marquis, Rachel Crothers, Augustus Thomas, and Sidney Howard, as well as several ministers including the Reverend John Haynes Holmes and Dr. Smith Ely Jelliffe, not only testified to the merits of the drama but also brought pressure upon the district attorney to reconsider the case. An investigating jury was organized and asked to review the drama. One juror said the audience needed more censorship than the play. Another thought *Desire Under the Elms* was a depressing tragedy but that it was not vulgar. The jury finally voted that the play should not be suppressed or even rewritten. The district attorney then allowed the drama to reopen, apparently with no changes in the script.

Desire Under the Elms, however, did run into more opposition in other cities. It was banned in Boston. When it was produced in Los Angeles, the cast was arrested and charged with performing in an obscene play. The drama was also banned in England.

When the Lord Chamberlain refused to license an American play, the success of its production in the United States often meant little to the British censor. On the other hand, when a foreign play that had been banned in England was successful in America, English producers usually asked the Lord Chamberlain to reconsider his decision. A typical example was *Young Woodley* by John Van Druten, a Welsh schoolteacher. When the Lord Chamberlain refused to license the play, English critics assumed that he had objected not only to some of the dialogue in which sex was discussed but also to the fact that the play dealt unfavorably with the English school system. Young Woodley, the central character, is an adolescent in an English boys' school who falls in love with the headmaster's wife. When the boys begin making slurring remarks about her, Woodley loses his temper, starts a fight with the ringleader, and is expelled.

Young Woodley opened in New York in 1925 without opposition from the protestors who had been investigating questionable dramas. Even during the tryout in Boston, there were only minor objections to the discussion of sex. Several lines of dialogue, which were deleted in Boston, were kept out of the play during the New York run. The American production, which owed much of its success to Glenn Hunter's sensitive portrayal of Woodley, strongly influenced Basil Dean, an English producer, who tried to persuade Lord Cromer, the Lord Chamberlain, to license the drama. For almost eighteen months Cromer refused to change his mind. The Stage society then gave a private club performance at the Arts Theater Club, and the critics, who wrote excellent reviews, said they could not understand why the play had been banned. Lord Cromer, who said he had read the manuscript three times, finally consented to attend a private club performance. Basil Dean later said that Cromer had been impressed by "the sincerity of our playing" and "the delicate way in which the theme had been handled." Lord Cromer asked for several cuts, and when these were made, he agreed to license the play for a London production. He also agreed to license a touring production if it were as well cast as the performance he had seen. When *Young Woodley* opened in London at the Savoy Theater, it became as substantial a success as it had been in the United States.

5

The Late 1920s

THE INVESTIGATING JURY organized in New York by the district attorney was inactive in the latter part of 1925. During this time, the popularity of censorable plays appeared to have abated. A few of the salacious shows were quick failures, not because they were immoral but simply because they were not well written or well acted. Early in 1926, the crusaders became aroused over such attractions as *The Shanghai Gesture* and *Lulu Belle* and asked the city officials to reactivate the jury.

The Shanghai Gesture by John Colton, which dealt with prostitution and drug addiction, starred Florence Reed as the proprietress of a notorious brothel. Twenty years earlier, she had been sold to Chinese junkmen when her lover, Sir Guy Charteris, had grown tired of her. To get revenge, she maneuvers to sell Charteris's daughter to the junkmen, but when she discovers that her own daughter, whom Charteris has raised, is a drug addict and a degenerate, she strangles her. Although critics in general objected to the lurid plot, they were impressed by Florence Reed's brilliant performance as the Chinese princess, Mother Goddam. The drama ran 208 performances but closed before the protestors completed a list of plays to be checked and before the district attorney reorganized the jury of investigators.

One of David Belasco's most controversial productions, *Lulu Belle* by Edward Sheldon and Charles MacArthur, had a longer run but was not investigated until the spring of 1927. Lenore Ulric starred as Lulu, a Harlem prostitute who lures George Randall away from his wife and children, leaves him for a prizefighter, and then deserts the fighter for another lover. When Lulu refuses to go back to George, he strangles her. The protestors were shocked not only by the flagrant immorality of the play but also by Miss Ulric's flamboyant performance and seductive costumes. By the time the investigating jurors went into action, however, *Lulu Belle* seemed mild in comparison to other salacious plays that were running.

Several other controversial dramas opened and closed before the investigation got under way. *The Virgin*, a combination of sex and religious fanaticism, ran only fifty-seven performances. A trumped-up, attempted seduction scene in *The Night Duel* failed to stimulate audience interest for more than seventeen performances. The district attorney's office, however, did take direct action against a revue, *Bunk of 1926*, that critics called tasteless and dull. The police ordered the revue padlocked, but the producers took the case to court and received a temporary injunction that permitted the show to reopen. The notoriety plus the fact that *Bunk of 1926* had been banned in Boston failed to stimulate box office sales, and the revue closed before any court action was taken on the injunction.

Agitators for reform were further aroused on February 22, 1926, when Earl Carroll threw a party after the evening's performance of *Vanities*. The *New York Daily Mirror* carried a story that while the guests were seated in the theater, a showgirl on stage stepped into a bathtub supposedly filled with champagne. Incensed crusaders demanded action, but federal authorities rather than the New York police immediately started an investigation and charged Earl Carroll with violation of the prohibition act. Although Carroll pleaded not guilty and said the tub had been filled with sherry and ginger ale, he was convicted for perjury, fined, and sentenced to serve a year and a day in the federal penitentiary in Atlanta. After four months and eleven days, he was released. Despite the adverse reaction from crusaders who demanded stricter censorship, the newspaper coverage brought Carroll favorable publicity and kept *Vanities* playing to large audiences for 390 performances.

The agitators for censorship increased their pressure on city officials in April, 1926, when *Sex,* a comedy by Jane Mast (pseudonym for Mae West) opened. Newspaper editors immediately joined the citizens' committees in the protest against "dirty shows," but the only direct action taken was the closing of *Bunk of 1926.*

An American Tragedy, a dramatization of Theodore Dreiser's novel by Patrick Kearney, which opened in October, 1926, followed Dreiser's story of Clyde Griffith who is accused of murdering the woman he seduced. Although he denies that he deliberately pushed her into the lake, the jury convicts him and he is electrocuted. The vice crusaders, ignoring the wide acclaim the novel had received, as well as the favorable reviews for the drama, included *An American Tragedy* in the list of offending plays to be investigated.

In December, Mayor James Walker, knowing that protests had reached Governor Alfred Smith, tried to avoid interference from Albany by contacting the major producers on Broadway and asking for their cooperation in cleaning up the theater. When no agreement could be reached on a workable plan, Governor Smith threatened to intercede. By January, the protestors were demanding that investigations be made of at least seven productions. Early in February, a rumor that Mae West intended to produce a drama about homosexuals, as well as the imminence of an investigation by Governor Smith, alerted New York officials to the need for quick action, and the district attorney's office closed three offending dramas: *The Captive, The Virgin Man,* and *Sex.* The police, accompanied by attorneys, photographers, newspaper reporters, and representatives from a citizens' committee, raided all three shows and arrested the producers and actors.

The Virgin Man, a farfetched comedy by William Francis Dugan about an innocent Yale student and three predatory women who try to seduce him, had run sixty-three performances before the raid. Jurors who tried *The Virgin Man* in special sessions sentenced the author and producer to serve jail terms and to pay fines of two hundred fifty dollars; the actors were given suspended sentences. In *Sex*, Mae West played Margie, a prostitute who is accused of robbery by a woman she had befriended. To get revenge, she seduces the woman's son and then threatens to marry him. As star, author, and coproducer of *Sex*, Miss West was fined five hundred dollars and sentenced to serve ten days in the workhouse.

In summarizing the crackdown by police, Ward Morehouse in *Matinee Tomorrow* called *Sex* trash but said *The Captive* was a powerful drama that should have been allowed to run without interference. *The Captive*, adapted by Arthur Hornblow, Jr., from the drama *La Prisonnière* by Edouard Bourdet, had been banned in England because it dealt with lesbianism, although the word *lesbian* was never used in the play. Helen Menken appeared as Irene, whose father tries to break up her friendship with a lesbian by sending her to Rome. In order to stay in Paris, Irene marries her childhood sweetheart, played by Basil Rathbone, but later deserts him to return to the other woman. *The Captive*, which many critics called a sensitive, restrained, psychological study, was condemned in New York for its implied degeneracy. The day after the raids, the actors and producers associated with *The Captive* were dismissed when the management agreed to close the drama. Gilbert Miller, the producing director, objected to this agreement because he thought he could win his case if it were tried in the courts. Famous Players-Lasky Motion Picture Company, which had a controlling interest in the plays Miller produced, overruled him, however, and forced him to keep the play closed. *The Captive*, however, had already caused a curious type of public reaction. In the play, as a means of getting messages to Irene, the other woman sent her a bouquet of violets. Even before the district attorney raided the show, a number of women had already refused to buy violets or even wear the color. As a result of the raids, closings, and fines imposed on *The Captive*, *The Virgin Man*, and *Sex*, other producers agreed to a self-censorship code, but their attempts to avoid friction with the police lasted only a few months.

In Philadelphia in 1927, city officials asked for a preliminary injunction to close *Revelry*, a drama by Maurine Watkins, adapted from the novel by Samuel Hopkins Adams, because it ridiculed the federal government and government agencies and exposed the corruption of important political figures. The play, supposedly fiction, dealt with a president of the United States who became involved with grafters and was driven to commit suicide. Although there was little doubt that the drama referred, in part, to the administration of the late President Warren G. Harding, Judge Robert H. Taulane in Common Pleas Court refused to grant the injunction, and the play continued its tryout in Philadelphia. Before the play opened in New York, the producer hoped the legal battle out of town would stimulate box office sales on Broadway, but the drama failed to interest New Yorkers and closed in six weeks.

After the agitation for censorship in 1927, the Wales Padlock Law was passed giving New York officials the authority to arrest and prosecute producers and actors associated with an immoral drama. The law further specified that if the producers were convicted, the theater in which the play had been presented would be padlocked for a year. District Attorneys Joab H. Banton of New York and Charles H. Dodd of Brooklyn had suggested the law and Senator B. Roger Wales had sponsored it in the legislature. Opponents of the bill felt that it gave too much power to the district attorney or assistant district attorney and therefore circulated a petition to repeal the law. The petition was sent to Governor Smith, but the law remained in effect until 1967.

The first drama to be affected by the law, *Maya* by Simon Gantillon, translated by Ernest Boyd, had been banned in England. The New York production opened late in February, 1928, with Aline MacMahon playing Bella, a prostitute in Marseilles, who symbolizes an illusion or a confidante to some men and a pathetic creature to others. When the district attorney began receiving protests about the drama, linking it to corruption in the theater, he sent one of his assistants to review *Maya*, in order to quash another concentrated crusade for censorship, and then, acting on the suggestion made in the assistant's report, closed the play after the fifteenth performance. The producers, knowing the Wales Padlock Law could close the theater for a year, did not appeal the case.

In the spring of 1928, the district attorney received strong protests against two dramas produced by the Theatre Guild; Eugene O'Neill's *Strange Interlude* and Ben Jonson's *Volpone*, as adapted by Stefan Zweig and translated by Ruth Langner. *Strange Interlude*, which had aroused reformers because it dealt with promiscuity, infidelity, and abortion, was the lengthiest drama produced in the United States up to that time. The Theatre Guild decided to try an innovation by offering it in one night with a playing time of more than four hours. Part one began at 5:15 P.M. and ran about two hours. The audience then had a dinner break of approximately one hour. Part two started at about 8:30 and ran a little longer than two and one half hours.

The plot, covering a period of twenty-five years, dealt with neurotic Nina Leeds, who had been promiscuous before marrying Sam Evans. When she becomes pregnant, her mother-in-law, Mrs. Evans, advises her to have an abortion because there is insanity in the Evans family. She has an affair with Dr. Darrell and gives birth to his son, but Sam thinks the child is his. Darrell and Nina, who have fallen in love, continue their affair, although they realize they cannot tell their son the truth about his parentage. When Sam dies, Darrell wants to marry Nina, but she settles down to an old-age marriage of convenience with Charlie Marsden, a lifelong friend.

Strange Interlude was to be remembered, not for its unusual length, but for O'Neill's use of soliloquies. During the normal dialogue, the actors spoke and moved naturally; during the soliloquies, in which they spoke their inner thoughts, all of the actors including the speaker remained motionless. This immobility made it easy for audiences to follow the transitions from dialogue to soliloquy. When *Strange Interlude* received the Pulitzer Prize for 1927–1928, a few critics disagreed with the award. Alexander Woollcott, the leading dissenter, called *Strange Interlude* the *"Abie's Irish Rose* of the pseudo-intelligentsia," but most of the critics endorsed the Pulitzer selection.

The banning of *Strange Interlude* in Boston did not come as a complete surprise, since the mayor of Boston had already banned *Desire Under the Elms. Strange Interlude* received additional publicity in Massachusetts, however, because the Theatre Guild, following the old custom of presenting entertainment outside the city limits, booked the drama into a theater in nearby Quincy, Massachusetts, where it prospered. A restaurant in Quincy, located near the theater, which did a highly profitable business during the dinner intermission for the play, was owned by Howard Johnson who later expanded his establishment into a national chain.

The Theatre Guild's production of *Volpone* had received excellent reviews, particularly for Dudley Digges's performance as Volpone, the moneylender who spreads the rumor that he is dying in order to induce potential heirs to shower him with gifts, and for Alfred Lunt's portrayal of Mosca, the crafty servant who outwits him. The vice crusaders had denounced *Volpone* for its immorality, especially for the scene in which the lecherous Volpone tried to rape Columba, the young wife of Corbaccio. The district attorney's reaction to complaints about *Strange Interlude* and *Volpone*, however, surprised the protestors, for he refused to interfere with the productions. Moreover, he said he had made this decision because he felt the Wales Padlock Law had not been passed to help over-zealous reformers condemn dramas with artistic merit and distinction.

Demands for censorship subsided during the summer and early fall until *The Pleasure Man*, originally called *The Drag*, opened in October, 1928. The drama, written by Mae West, who did not appear in the production, made pointed references to an off-stage episode in which a promiscuous actor is castrated and dies, and also included a drag party to which homosexuals came dressed as women. Pro-testors had little time to demand action from the district attorney, for he moved quickly, closed the production after the second per-formance, and arrested the entire cast.

In 1929, New York producers, alarmed over the steady decline in theater attendance, blamed the competition of talking pictures, the higher operating costs, the higher ticket prices, the rudeness of box office men, and the monopolistic speculators who controlled the best tickets. Reformers, on the other hand, continued to protest to the district attorney for stronger censorship and insisted that a great many people had stopped going to the theater because they objected to the decadence in the drama.

Late in 1929, producers Arthur Hopkins, Brock Pemberton, and Gilbert Miller formed the League of New York Theaters to fight speculators who controlled blocks of seats for successful shows and were charging exorbitant fees. In July, 1930, the League, whose membership now included ticket brokers, theater owners, and mana-gers, drew up an agreement to turn over blocks of seats to ac-credited brokers who were to charge a maximum of seventy-five cents per ticket. At the same time, manager-members were to keep a per-centage of the best seats on sale at the box office. The League hired a manager who tried to put the plan into operation, but speculators who were not members brought an injunction against the League claiming that it was restricting trade. Arguments also developed within the League, for several producers insisted that they had to presell tickets to speculators to help recover investment costs. Within a short time, all brokers withdrew from the League, and by the end of the season, the League could not cope with its mounting problems. The League did succeed, however, in helping to stop the enactment of legislation for censorship, which was under consideration in Albany, by agreeing to act as its own censor and to take whatever action might be necessary against any production that the members felt offended the public.

6

The 1930s

WHEN *Lysistrata* by Aristophanes, adapted by Gilbert Seldes and presented by the Philadelphia Theater Association, opened in June, 1930, a few vice crusaders objected to the bawdy plot dealing with Lysistrata who leads a peace movement by convincing the women of Greece not to sleep with their husbands until the wars are ended. The New York officials, however, took no action against the fast-paced comedy skillfully staged by Norman Bel Geddes. On the other hand, censorship was still a major problem, particularly for musical revues that featured nudity and raffish humor. Shortly after Earl Carroll's *Vanities* opened on July 1, 1930, the New York police closed the show on charges of excessive vulgarity in several sketches and a charge of indecency against Faith Bacon, a dancer, whose costume consisted of one small fan. After Carroll toned down the sketches and gave Miss Bacon a larger fan, the police permitted *Vanities* to reopen.

During the latter part of 1931, a new censorship problem developed. The Minsky Brothers took over the Central Theater on Broadway and the Republic Theater on Forty-second Street to present burlesque shows that featured stripteasers and rowdy, unsubtle comedy. The owners of other theaters in this Broadway sector, who foresaw the deterioration of their property, went to court to stop the Minsky Brothers. While the owners waited for their case to come to trial, the Minsky shows continued and the property values dropped. It was not until 1939 that burlesque shows were officially banned in New York.

Tobacco Road by Jack Kirkland, based on Erskine Caldwell's novel, loomed as a failure in 1933, for it opened to poor reviews, although a few critics qualified their negative comments by adding that Henry Hull gave a compelling performance in an unsavory drama. Hull played Jeeter Lester, a lecherous Georgia cracker who lives on land his family had rented for many years. His dim-witted son Dude marries Sister Bessie, a lustful evangelist old enough to be his mother. Jeeter trades his oldest daughter, Pearl, to a neighbor for a sack of turnips, but when Pearl runs away, Jeeter's wife tells him that Pearl was not his daughter. As the sordid drama ends, Jeeter's mother has wandered off to die, and Jeeter knows the bank officials will put him off the land.

Audience response was definitely negative, for *Tobacco Road* shocked many theatergoers with its earthiness. In his history of the American drama, Arthur Hobson Quinn referred to *Tobacco Road* as "probably the depths of degradation to which the drama may descend," and condemned it for its "lack of any significance in the characters or situations." The play might have run into censorship problems, but sociologists began pointing out that it was a realistic portrait of life among impoverished whites in Georgia; Burns Mantle wrote a special column in which he commented that *Tobacco Road*, despite its sordidness, had social significance. To keep the play running, the cast, under the leadership of Henry Hull, agreed to take salary cuts and work for Equity minimum salaries. Attendance did not pick up, however, until Matthew Zimmerman, head of the Leblang cut-rate ticket agency, took over the production and built it into a popular cut-rate success with a top price of $1.50.

After Henry Hull left the cast, his replacement, James Barton, scored a personal triumph as Jeeter, as did other actors who succeeded Barton. Although *Tobacco Road* originally had been a serious drama, actors began playing it for laughs by emphasizing the lusty scenes and earthy dialogue. The play ran during the summers of 1934 and 1935 when the number of attractions in New York dropped to new lows. By the end of its fifth year, *Tobacco Road* had surpassed the run of *Abie's Irish Rose*, which had established the previous record for longevity. *Tobacco Road* finally closed in New York after 3,182 consecutive performances, a record broken by only one play, *Life With Father*, and one musical, *Fiddler on the Roof*.

Tobacco Road was highly successful on the road where it drew larger grosses than in New York, and the longer the play continued on Broadway, the higher the interest mounted on the road. The drama, however, also ran into problems with censors outside New York and was banned in several cities. As late as 1950, the play had not been performed in several states including Maine, Vermont, New Hampshire, Rhode Island, and Florida. In Chicago, during the 1935–1936 season, when Mayor Edward Kelly saw *Tobacco Road* after it had been running for five weeks, he called it "a mass of filth and indecency," and immediately canceled the theater's license. The producers were able to get a temporary injunction preventing the mayor from stopping the play, but the case was taken to the United States Circuit Court of Appeals, which upheld the mayor's decree and made the injunction null and void. Several liberal groups registered strong protests against the ban, but Mayor Kelly refused to allow the play to reopen. *Tobacco Road*, curiously enough, was the first play to be banned in Chicago since 1929 when the censors had closed *Frankie and Johnny*, also written by Jack Kirkland.

They Shall Not Die, *Within the Gates*, *The Children's Hour*, *Till the Day I Die*, and *Waiting for Lefty* were all banned in England, but they were produced in New York in 1934 and 1935 without any official interference. In other cities in the United States, however, they met with opposition from censors.

In February, 1934, the Theatre Guild produced *They Shall Not Die*, a drama by John Wexley based on a trial held in Scottsboro, Alabama, in 1931. Two white girls had accused nine Negro boys of rape while they were all riding in a freight train, and the trial brought death sentences for eight of the boys. The case was appealed to the United States Supreme Court and, based on charges against the manner in which the verdict had been reached, the Supreme Court ordered a new trial in 1932. This time one girl changed her testimony and only one boy was sentenced. Again the case went to the Supreme Court which ordered a new trial because Negroes had not been accepted for the jury. At the second retrial, four of the boys were sentenced to life imprisonment and charges against the other five boys were dropped. When *They Shall Not Die* opened, John Wexley said his characters were fictional, but critics pointed out that Wexley had used the same factual material as Langston Hughes who had written the drama *Scottsboro Limited* in 1932. Many of the New York critics disapproved of *They Shall Not Die* because they felt that Wexley, instead of proving his point that the boys were falsely convicted, emphasized the plight of their attorney. To the critics, therefore, the drama lacked conviction. The play ran sixty-two performances in New York with no apparent opposition, but when it was scheduled to open in Newark, New Jersey, the city officials branded it as communist propaganda and banned the play.

Within the Gates by Sean O'Casey, which opened in 1934, was set in England. In this symbolic drama, a poet imagines that a dream world exists in Hyde Park where he meets a bishop, a harlot, and radicals who argue about God and religion. The play puzzled some audiences and disturbed others but it also had enthusiastic supporters. After a run of 101 performances, the drama was sent to Boston to begin a road tour, but several religious groups in Boston protested against the drama to the mayor, claiming that *Within the Gates* held religion up to ridicule. The mayor of Boston agreed with the protestors that the drama degraded religion and closed the show. In the *New York Times* for May 27, 1935, Brooks Atkinson reprimanded the Boston clerics for calling the play antireligious when "they mean it is anti-church." Atkinson also said that *Within the Gates* was "the most religious play the modern drama has produced" and that it was banned by "a handful of misguided clergymen." The producers, however, rather than gamble on similar negative reaction and possible banning in other cities, brought *Within the Gates* back to New York for a limited run.

Lillian Hellman had based *The Children's Hour*, a drama which rocked the theatrical world when it opened in November, 1934, on a nineteenth-century case that included a reference to lesbianism as a cause for libel and was tried in the courts of Scotland. Instead of hedging, Miss Hellman treated the discussion of lesbianism frankly, but she also developed the theme that innocent people could be ruined by vicious, slanderous lies. Mary Tilford, a malicious child who attends a private school run by Karen Wright and Martha Dobie, is trapped in a series of lies and punished. In retaliation, she insinuates to her grandmother that Karen and Martha are lesbians. When the scandalized grandmother notifies all parents to withdraw their daughters and forces the school to close, Karen and Martha file a libel suit against her but lose the case. In the last act, the grandmother, who has learned that Mary has lied, comes to make amends, but Martha, after admitting that Mary's accusation, although false, could have been based on truth, has committed suicide.

Even though the critics pointed out that the third act was developed by a series of anticlimaxes, they still rated *The Children's Hour* as the most vigorous drama of the season. It was rumored to be the leading contender for the Pulitzer Prize, but at the end of the 1934–1935 season, it received the same form of censorship given *What Price Glory?*, for the Pulitzer Committee bypassed *The Children's Hour* and selected *The Old Maid* by Zoe Akins as the prize-winning drama. The announcement of the award caused the most vehement series of protests in the history of the Pulitzer drama awards. Objectors called the selection disgraceful, claiming that *The Old Maid* had been the worst choice the Pulitzer Committee had made up to that time, and accused the Pulitzer Board of acting as censors by rejecting Lillian Hellman's drama because of its immorality. The Board explained that *The Children's Hour* was not an original drama, because it was based on a court trial, and therefore was ineligible for the prize. The critics, in turn, said that *The Old Maid* should also have been declared ineligible because it was based on a novel by Edith Wharton. The controversy incensed the critics sufficiently to reactivate the New York Drama Critics Circle the following year in order to award its own prizes. *The Children's Hour* had no official interference in New York where it not only ran 691 performances but also survived the summer of 1935 when the number of attractions on Broadway dropped to a new low of four. On the road, however, it met with official censorship, for it was banned in such cities as Chicago and Boston. It was also banned in England.

In March, 1935, the Group Theater presented a double bill of two short plays, *Till the Day I Die* and *Waiting for Lefty* by Clifford Odets. *Till the Day I Die* dealt with a young German, the leader of a revolt against Hitler, who is captured and tortured to reveal the names of his accomplices. He commits suicide to avoid giving any information, but his associates, not knowing of his sacrifice, think he has betrayed them. The second play, *Waiting for Lefty*, dealt with a taxidriver's union that is controlled by union officers, labor racketeers, and radicals who try to prevent a strike. The workers are waiting for a delegate named Lefty before they vote on a walkout, and when they learn that Lefty has been killed, they begin shouting, "Strike! Strike!"

Neither of the two plays had any apparent problems with censors in New York, but *Waiting for Lefty*—which some local officials outside of New York thought might be considered communist propaganda—was banned in a number of cities including Laguna Beach, Chelsea, Philadelphia, and Bridgeport. The school board in New Haven, after granting permission for the play to be staged, reconsidered and refused to let *Waiting for Lefty* be performed in a public school building. The play was also banned at the Yale Drama School, but the ban was lifted sometime later. In Boston, an official censor attended the opening performance; within the next few days, the theater manager, after talking to the police, was ready to evict the actors. The censor, however, took definite action by ordering the play to be closed, and the police arrested four members of the cast on charges of "using profanity in a public assembly." Attorneys for the actors were able to have the trial postponed, and, several weeks later, in spite of the official ban, the play was reopened, with the profanity deleted from the script.

In 1934, political groups that felt that too many American actors were out of work, began protesting against the increasing number of English dramas that were being produced in the United States with all-British casts. Attempts to pressure Congress into passing a bill to bar foreign actors from appearing in American productions unless they were essential to the drama, however, were unsuccessful. American dramatists joined the protest against foreign actors and plays in 1935, when the Theatre Guild presented Elisabeth Bergner, an Austrian actress heralded in Europe as another Sarah Bernhardt, making her American debut in *Escape Me Never* by Margaret Kennedy, an English dramatist. The American reviewers did not echo the European critics in calling Miss Bergner a great actress, but they did praise her portrayal of Gemma, a young girl who has an illegitimate child. She finds a new lover, Sebastian, who is unfaithful to her, but when her child dies, Gemma and Sebastian realize they cannot leave each other. On the opening night, two American dramatists, Paul Sifton and Virgil Geddes, along with their wives, picketed the theater and distributed circulars condemning the Theatre Guild for its unfairness to American dramatists, because their plays, which the Guild had accepted, had been put aside to give preference to *Escape Me Never*. The picketing continued for several nights but did not affect attendance, for interest in seeing Miss Bergner kept *Escape Me Never* playing to capacity houses until she decided she needed a rest and the drama was forced to close after ninety-six performances.

New York almost had a strict censorship law in 1937, for the Dunnigan Bill, which would have given the city license commissioner the power to revoke a license if he thought a show was immoral, was passed by the New York legislature and was ready for Governor Lehman's signature. A group of prominent actors, producers, and writers led a protest, claiming that the bill gave too much power to one official. They carried their fight to Albany and continued their protest until the governor vetoed the bill.

A lawsuit in the late 1930s made many of the producers and dramatists who were opposed to censorship in any form realize that the English system of censorship, despite its many disadvantages, at least protected writers and managers from libel suits. Under the English system, once the Lord Chamberlain had issued a license for a play, the government was basically responsible for any legal controversy that might arise, particularly if people who were still alive or their families objected to the manner in which they were represented on the stage. Since the United States, on the other hand, had no official censorship, dramatists and producers could be sued for libel. *The Masque of Kings* by Maxwell Anderson, produced by the Theatre Guild in 1937, was another version of the Mayerling tragedy and the suicide pact of Crown Prince Rudolph of Hapsburg and young Baroness Mary Vetsera. Approximately one month after the play opened, Anderson was accused of distorting historical events and personalities to suit his purposes. The Archduke of Tuscany, one of Anderson's villains in the play, had a son living in New York who protested against the characterization of his father as a conspirator in the play, but before he could take legal action, another suit for twenty-five thousand dollars was filed by a countess who claimed that she had been depicted unfavorably and her privacy violated by *The Masque of Kings*. The Theatre Guild and Maxwell Anderson settled her case out of court and apparently reached an agreement with the son of the Archduke. Although the American playwrights saw the advantage of this one phase of the English system of censorship, they still preferred the American system because they knew the Lord Chamberlain would refuse to license a play, regardless of how well written it was, if he could not get approval from the people depicted or from surviving members of their families.

George Jean Nathan believed that critics, at times, could be more effective than censors in closing a drama that offended theatergoers. To prove his point, he cited the case of *Tortilla Flat*, a drama based on John Steinbeck's novel, produced in New York in 1938. Jack Kirkland, who wrote the adaptation, emphasized the earthiness of the story but did not include the quality that had given the novel its distinction—Steinbeck's compassion for his characters. Almost every New York critic denounced the play, which closed after five performances. According to Nathan, Kirkland, incensed by the brutal reviews, followed one critic, Richard Watts of the *Herald Tribune*, into a bar and started a fight. In a very short time, Kirkland was knocked out and had to be carried back to his hotel. Nathan concluded his story with the comment that if *Tortilla Flat* had been condemned by the censors rather than the critics it would probably have had a longer run.

Broadway producers still considered Boston to be a good tryout city in the 1930s, even though they were never certain what action the censor might take. *American Landscape*, by Elmer Rice, which tried out in Boston in 1938, combined history, fantasy, and realism in the story of Captain Dale, who plans to sell his large estate to a German-American bund which will use it for a Nazi camp. The ghosts of his ancestors and other prominent Americans come back to earth to argue with him. Before he can complete the sale, Dale dies of a stroke and his heirs decide to keep the property in the family. John Spencer, the official theatrical censor in Boston, ordered the show closed unless the profanity in the dialogue was deleted. When *American Landscape* opened in New York without interference or restrictions, it again proved George Jean Nathan's theory that critics could be more effective than censors, for the bland reviews killed audience interest and the play closed after a short run of forty-three performances.

7

The WPA Federal
Theater Project

THE EXPERIMENT of government-supported theater had a short but turbulent existence. In 1935, when Harry Hopkins, head of the WPA relief program, asked Hallie Flanagan, director of plays at Vassar, to head the theater program, which had the approval of both President and Mrs. Franklin Roosevelt, she accepted. She took office as director in August and arranged for conferences in Washington and New York with representative playwrights, producers, heads of theatrical unions, and directors from college and community theaters. By October she had set up her program on a regional basis with plans for active, full-scale production in 1936.

Almost from the start, the project ran into difficulties, for problems of restrictions, diplomacy, liaison with commercial producers, and government censorship developed in the WPA project in New York. The United States government was soon placed in the paradoxical position of banning productions that it had subsidized.

Elmer Rice, who had agreed to head the New York division, selected *Ethiopia*, which dealt with the conflict between Italy and Ethiopia, as his first production. Several officials in Washington were dubious about the drama because it included references to Mussolini and Haile Selassie. They felt that since Rice's production was government-sponsored, its presentation could lead to serious political implications. Elmer Rice insisted that there must be no censorship or interference with his productions, regardless of how controversial they might be, and when he was not guaranteed that he would have this freedom, he resigned in January, 1936. Philip W. Barber, who was appointed to replace him, canceled *Ethiopia.*

Since the purpose of the WPA project was to provide work for unemployed actors, technicians, writers, and directors during the depression, the New York critics tempered their reviews for the first few WPA productions, which opened in February, 1936. One of the more interesting of these productions, *American Holiday* by Edwin L. and Albert Barker, was said to have been based on reactions in Flemington, New Jersey, where Bruno Hauptmann was tried for the Lindbergh kidnapping. The drama showed how a small town suffered from the effects of a murder trial when the newspapers publicized the crime as though it were a national scandal, and news correspondents, photographers, and curiosity seekers crowded into the small community.

The Living Newspaper Unit planned to present a series of productions comprised of news sketches written by reporters and dramatized by a group of playwrights headed by Arthur Laurents. The first Living Newspaper, *Triple A Plowed Under*, which Philip Barber had selected as a substitute for *Ethiopia*, opened in March and dealt with such topics as war, inflation, milk prices, drought, sharecroppers, and soil conservation. The second Living Newspaper, *1935*, opened in May and included references to Hauptmann, Huey Long, John Lewis, and Barbara Hutton.

The WPA theater project demonstrated that it could handle controversial dramas, for in October, 1936, it presented a dramatization of Sinclair Lewis's novel *It Can't Happen Here,* adapted by John C. Moffitt and Sinclair Lewis. The play illustrated how Hitler's tactics could operate in America by developing the story of a president of the United States who sets up a fascist regime and organizes his Corpos Guards. A newspaper editor who openly denounces the Fascists is thrown into a concentration camp. He escapes, goes to Canada, and plans to continue his fight to save America. *It Can't Happen Here* attracted attention across the country, for the WPA presented it on a national scale by opening it simultaneously in seventeen cities that had WPA theater projects.

By the end of 1936, managers of commercial theaters in New York were grumbling about the competition from WPA projects, although, in reality, the federal programs were competing mainly with low-priced revivals. In other cities, WPA projects ran into problems because regular theatergoers seldom attended performances, and the low price scale, which ranged from twenty-five to fifty-five cents a ticket, did not draw as many new patrons as the managements had anticipated.

Official censorship from Washington stopped another WPA production, *The Cradle Will Rock* by Marc Blitzstein, in June, 1937. The plot concerned steel workers who try to form a union and are opposed by Mr. Mister, a ruthless capitalist who controls the town, the press, and the church. He organizes a committee to destroy the union and makes plans to have the labor organizer assassinated, but the union finally wins. On the opening night, just a few hours before the performance was to begin, the play was banned by the WPA Federal Theater Project on an order from Washington, D.C., officials. After the audience arrived at the Maxine Elliott Theater, several members of the cast presented an improvised entertainment while other members scouted the neighborhood to find an empty theater and finally discovered that the Venice Theater was available. Since the WPA

The Ziegfeld Follies aroused the public in the World War I era and the early 1920s with its scantily clad showgirls. Ann Pennington (left), a featured Ziegfeld performer famous for her legs and dimpled knees, once startled *Follies* audiences by burlesquing a famous nude painting. Yvonne Grey (right) was one of many beautiful *Follies* girls photographed in minimal costumes. The near-nudity of some musical shows led to police checks and court action in several cities.

A breakthrough in realistic war dramas came in 1924, with the success of *What Price Glory?* by Maxwell Anderson and Lawrence Stallings. At top, Louis Wolheim (center) as Captain Flagg, William Boyd as Sergeant Quirt, with Leyla Georgie as Charmaine. Below, Cognac Pete (Luis Alberni), Charmaine's father, comes to headquarters to accuse Sergeant Quirt, seated at table, of having ruined his daughter. Captain Flagg looks on at right. The earthy, realistic dialogue led to the play's rejection by the Pulitzer Prize Committee, which had considered *What Price Glory?* for its annual award.

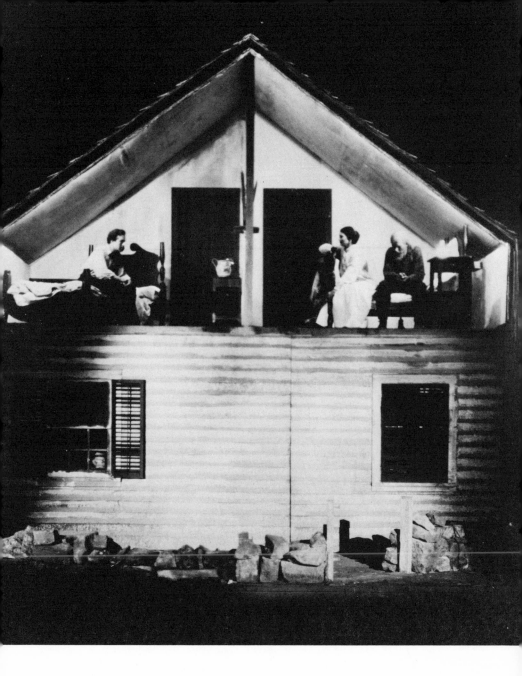

The ingenious set for Eugene O'Neill's *Desire under the Elms.* Although morals crusaders succeeded in having the play closed, protests by prominent people in the arts resulted in the ban's being lifted. The set was so constructed that action could take place in different rooms of the house simultaneously. Shown here on the second floor: Charles Ellis as Eben Cabot, in love with his stepmother Abbie, played by Mary Morris, with Walter Huston as the aged Ephraim Cabot.

Two plays produced in 1926 aroused the vice crusaders. *Lulu Belle*, written by Edward Sheldon and Charles MacArthur and starring Lenore Ulric and Henry Hull in a David Belasco production, dealt with a Harlem prostitute who lures a man away from his wife and children and then deserts him (above). *The Shanghai Gesture* by John Colton is the lurid story of Mother Goddam, a Chinese princess, who seeks revenge on the lover who sold her to Chinese junkmen. Above right, McKay Morris as Sir Guy Charteris, the former lover, Florence Reed as Mother Goddam, and one of the caged girls in her brothel. Below right, Mother Goddam showing off her gallery of laughing dolls, where the caged girls are on view.

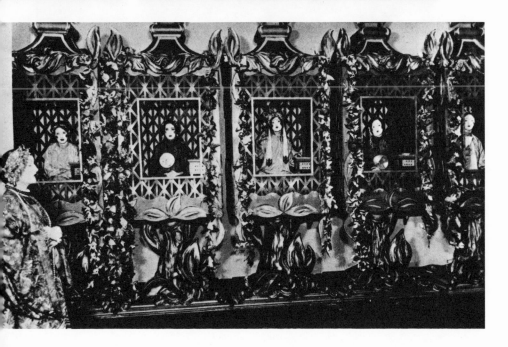

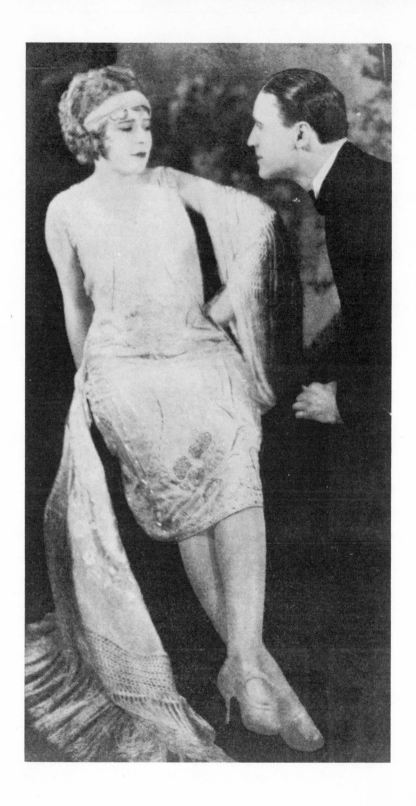

Mae West had one of her most notorious successes in the 1926 comedy drama *Sex* by Jane Mast (a pseudonym for the star herself). The police, well covered by the press and accompanying attorneys, closed the play and arrested the performers. Mae West is shown (facing page) with Lyons Wickland in a scene from *Sex* and, above, in court during a hearing after her arrest.

"Banned in Boston" was to become a familiar phrase during the 1920s. This time the victim was Eugene O'Neill's provocative four-hour drama *Strange Interlude,* which opened instead in nearby Quincy, Massachusetts, where it prospered. Shown above is the original cast in the Theatre Guild production: Glenn Anders, Lynn Fontanne, Tom Powers, and Earle Larimore. At left, Lynn Fontanne and Earle Larimore. The play received the Pulitzer Prize for 1927–28.

Waiting for Lefty was one of a Group Theater production of two short plays by Clifford Odets. The scene above shows cab drivers taking a union strike vote. Calling his fellow workers to action is Elia Kazan, center, with arms raised. Untroubled in New York, the play was banned in a number of cities, including Boston, where it was permitted to reopen after profanity was deleted from the script.

The Children's Hour by Lillian Hellman was rumored to be the leading contender for the Pulitzer Prize for 1934–35, but it was by-passed, presumably because it dealt with charges of lesbianism. The play was banned in Chicago and Boston, but its supporters in New York and elsewhere denounced the Pulitzer Prize Committee for cowardice and censorship. Shown at right are Florence McGee, Anne Revere, and Katherine Emery in the original New York production.

Slum Housing Dramatized; President Suggested Title

How one-third of the nation lives.

The Living Newspaper production of *One Third of a Nation* (playbill above) was one of the most successful of the WPA theater presentations during the 1930s. Its detractors denounced the use of federal funds to create support, as they saw it, for President Roosevelt's New Deal. The impressive set for the play was designed by Howard Bay, representing four stories of a tenement showing ill-kept rooms and fire-trap staircases. The scene at left is the play's climax, with smoke pouring forth and lights being played on the front of the house.

Below, entrance to Minsky's Burlesque, one of the theaters closed by New York police in 1939. Mayor Fiorello LaGuardia officially banned all burlesque shows in the city.

At right, playbills of two productions staged by Orson Welles for the WPA Federal Theater Project. *Macbeth* interested critics because the play was set in the West Indies without changing the text. The program shown here for *The Cradle Will Rock* was never used. Just a few hours before the first performance was to begin, the play was banned by order of officials in Washington, D.C. Welles and producer John Houseman (both of whose names are misspelled in the playbill) left the WPA project and founded the Mercury Theater, which later presented the Blitzstein play.

Broadway producers objected to such WPA Federal Theater productions as *Murder in the Cathedral,* seeing them as unfair competition. The T. S. Eliot drama was highly successful as a WPA production (above) at very low ticket prices. When it was revived commercially in 1938 with a top of $3.00, it ran for only twenty-one performances.

Lafayette Theatre

2225 SEVENTH AVENUE

Phone: TIllinghast 5-1424   **New York City**

FIRE NOTICE: The exit, indicated by a red light and sign, nearest to the seat you occupy, is the shortest route to the street. In the event of fire or other emergency, please do not run—WALK TO THAT EXIT. JOHN J. McELLIGOTT, *Fire Chief and Commissioner*

THE NEGRO THEATRE

A W. P. A. FEDERAL THEATRE

Presents

"𝔐𝔞𝔠𝔟𝔢𝔱𝔥"

BY

WILLIAM SHAKESPEARE

Arranged and Staged by ORSON WELLES

Costumes and Settings by NAT KARSON

Lighting by Feder

The Federal Theatre Project is part of the W. P. A. program. However, the viewpoint expressed in this play is not necessarily that of the W. P. A. or any other agency of the Government

The Negro Theatre is also under the sponsorship of the New York Urban League

---

THE THEATRE

FEDERAL · USA · WORK PROGRAM WPA **THEATRE**

HALLIE FLANAGAN   PHILIP W. BARBER
Director   *Dir. of Productions for N. Y. C.*

PROJECT 891

John Housman, Producer

PRESENTS

THE CRADLE WILL ROCK

By

MARC BLITZSTEIN

Production by ORSON WELLS
Conductor, LEHMAN ENGEL

Sets and Costumes by ED SCHRUERS
Lighting by FEDER
Associate Producer, TED THOMAS

THE CAST

The Moll	Olive Stanton
A Gent	George Fairchild
A Dick	Guido Alexander
A Cop	Robert Worth
Clerk	Clifford Mack
Members of The Liberty Committee:	
Editor Daily	Bert Weston
Prexie	Hansford Wilson
Yasha	Edward Fuller
Dauber	Warren Goddard
Dr. Specialist	Frank Marvel
Rev. Salvation	Edward Hemmer
Druggist	John Adair
Mr. Mister	Will Geer
Mrs. Mister	Peggy Coudray
Junior Mister	Hiram Sherman

Sister Mister	Dulce Fox
Maid	Josephine Heathman
Steve	Howard Bird
Bugs	Geoffrey Powers
Gus	George Fairchild
Sadie	Marion Grant Rudley
Larry	Howard da Silva
Prof. Skoot	Hiram Sherman
Prof. Mamie	Leopold Badia
Prof. Trixie	George Smithfield
Reporters	Robert Hopkins, Huntley Weston and Jack Mealy
Ella Hammer	Blanche Collins

Henry Colker, Rose Cooper, Georgia Empey, Harriett Flammang, Mary Kukawski, Donnald MacMillan, Jane D. Madison, Lillian Sheldon, Paul Varro, Ann Voorhees, Wallace Acton, Peter Barbier, Cora Burler, Solomon Goldstein, Edith Groome, Don Harwood, Frank Kelly, Paula Laurence, Elizabeth Malone, Aurelia Molnar, Walter Palm, Myron Paulson, Louis Pennewell, Helena Rapport, Henry Russelle, Nina Salama, Bernard Savage, Harry Singer, Raymond Tobin, Charles Uday, Richie White and Jay Wilson.

ORCHESTRA

WPA Federal Theatre Orchestra

Associate Conductor, ALEX SARON

PRODUCTION STAFF

General Stage Manager	William L. Greenbaum
Asst. Tech. Directors	Carol King and Walter Leroy
Stage Managers	Charles Pittenger, David Clark and Marga Herdegen
Costumes executed by	Paul Clifford
Scenery executed by	WPA Federal Theatre Workshop
Sound supervised by	Vincent Mallory

Dept. of Information—122 East 42nd St.—MUrray Hill 4-5900

A life-size photograph of Nejla Ates (left) doing her belly dance in *Fanny* in 1954 was displayed in front of the theater showing the S. N. Behrman-Joshua Logan-Harold Rome musical. As the run progressed Miss Ates discarded bits of her abbreviated costume, leading to a police warning that the show would be closed unless she desisted. *Fanny* had a good run.

Hair—"The American Tribal Love Rock Musical" by Gerome Ragni, James Rado, and Galt MacDermot—finally broke all barriers on Broadway in 1968. After a successful run off Broadway, the teen-age love story celebrating the revolt of youth against establishment values opened to mixed reviews, but drew capacity audiences and became an international success. The original cast is pictured below celebrating the show's second anniversary.

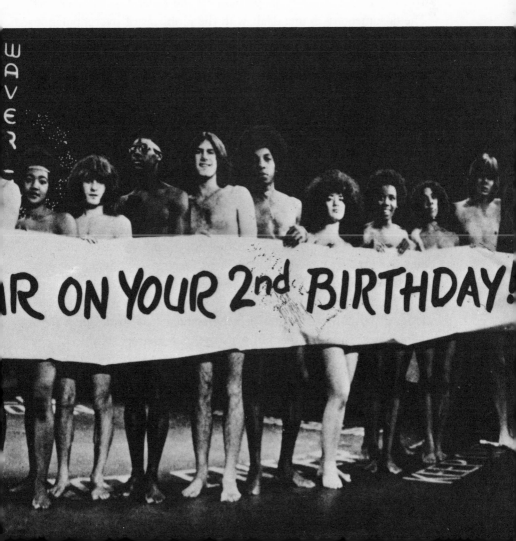

project had paid for the scenery and costumes, John Houseman and Orson Welles, who produced *The Cradle Will Rock*, presented it on a bare stage in concert style with Marc Blitzstein playing the piano accompaniment. In protest against the banning from Washington, Houseman and Welles left the WPA project, founded the Mercury Theater, and reopened *The Cradle Will Rock* as a Mercury production in December. In January, 1938, Sam H. Grisman took over *The Cradle Will Rock* and presented it at the Windsor Theater for an additional run.

Unofficial censorship from Washington developed in connection with the WPA production of *One Third of a Nation*, presented in 1938 by the Living Newspaper Unit of the Federal Theater project. The documentary drama dealt with the problems of overpopulation, rent strikes, epidemics, plagues, and inadequate housing facilities in the tenements. The title was taken from President Franklin D. Roosevelt's second inaugural address in which he said that one third of the nation is "ill-housed, ill-clad, and ill-nourished."

As a focal character, the writers used a man interested in building a housing development in a slum district. By asking questions, he discovers that if he builds an apartment house for low income families, he will be paying commissions that will force him to charge more than three times the rentals he had originally planned; that the financing he would get from the government would cover only a small percentage of the costs; and that the institutions that owned the inadequate, ill-kept tenement buildings and were responsible for the poor housing included a prominent, wealthy church. The drama, which offered no solution to the problems, received excellent reviews for its smooth staging, provocative ideas, and impressive stage set designed by Howard Bay, which represented four stories of a tenement house showing the filthy rooms and firetrap staircases. The success of the production, which ran 273 performances, stirred up politicians in Washington, particularly those who were opposed to the entire WPA theater project. They protested that the play was using federal funds to give supporters of Roosevelt's New Deal policy additional publicity, but their efforts to stop *One Third of a Nation* from continuing its run were unsuccessful.

The politicians were not alone in protesting against the management of the WPA theater project. Directors of WPA productions objected to government censorship. Actors Equity on several occasions set up picket lines to protest against amateurs being hired when professional actors were still unemployed. In its 1937 report, the Federal Theater had estimated that its productions were playing to an average of three hundred fifty thousand people each week in twenty-seven states. By 1938, many Broadway producers, convinced that the WPA Federal Theater had become a serious threat to the commercial theater, protested against the government's subsidizing attractions that provided unfair competition, since the WPA admission prices were far lower than those charged by commercial theaters. The original WPA production of T. S. Eliot's *Murder in the Cathedral* in 1936, for example, had been very successful, but a commercial revival of the drama in 1938 with a top price of three dollars failed after twenty-one performances.

The reverse was true of *Johnny Johnson* by Pulitzer Prize dramatist Paul Green. The play presented the tragedy of an honest man who finds he has no place in a society dominated by dishonest opportunists. When he fights against Germany in World War I, he gets into trouble with his superior officers. The girl he loves is sent to an insane asylum, and as the play ends, Johnny sees the world preparing for another war. Although the commercial production of *Johnny Johnson* in New York was a serious contender for the Critics Circle Award in 1936–1937, it failed after a run of sixty-eight performances. On the other hand, it was very successful in cities on the west coast where it was presented as a Federal Theater production.

Broadway producers also argued that the government subsidy

for WPA productions enabled technicians and directors to experiment with new plays, new lighting devices, and new methods of staging that would involve too great a risk for the commercial theater. This experimentation was particularly evident in two productions associated with Orson Welles. *Macbeth*, which Welles arranged for the Federal Theater Negro Unit, opened in April, 1936. The production was an unusual, imaginative version of the tragedy, for without changing the text, Welles set the play in the West Indies and capitalized on the setting by having the cast wear colorful West Indian costumes. Among the effective scenes were those involving the witches, which took place in the jungle. In January, 1937, when the WPA Theater produced a revival of Christopher Marlowe's *Dr. Faustus*, Orson Welles received glowing reviews not only for his performance as Faustus but also for his unusual staging. Welles used a bare stage that had trapdoors and hidden staircases for mysterious entrances and exists. Instead of scenery, he made effective use of special lights, spotlights, and beams of smoke. Mephistopheles, for example, seemed to emerge from a ball of fire and billowing smoke. When Faustus was to disappear, Mephistopheles snapped his fingers, a puff of smoke came up, and Faustus quickly vanished through a trapdoor. In addition to the recognition it brought Welles, *Dr. Faustus* also made critics aware of Abe Feder, who was responsible for the unusual lighting effects. *Dr. Faustus* ran 128 performances but could have drawn large audiences much longer. The crowded WPA Theater schedule, however, forced *Dr. Faustus* to close to make way for other dramas which were waiting for available WPA theaters.

By June, 1939, when the WPA theater project was completing its original three-year schedule, supporters of the project lobbied to have funds allocated so that the Federal Theater would continue. At the same time, opposing politicians, who claimed that left wing actors and radical plays were dominating the program, started an investigation. Unfavorable testimony and opposition to the WPA project presented to the House Committee investigating un-American activities led to the termination of the WPA Federal Theater on July 11, 1939. During its three years of existence, it had provided work for approximately thirteen thousand actors, directors, and technicians, and had produced approximately twelve thousand plays.

8

The 1940s

TRYOUTS of controversial dramas in Boston in the 1940s still involved the risk of official censorship as well as audience disapproval. *Battle of the Angels* by Tennessee Williams, which the Theatre Guild opened in Boston in 1940, dealt with a woman who uses the back room of her shop for trysts with lovers while her paralyzed husband is confined upstairs. The opening performance was a fiasco, for the audience laughed during scenes that were meant to be serious. The Boston censor did not find the audience reaction amusing, for he not only denounced the drama but also threatened to close it unless several scenes were rewritten. Even more important, many Bostonians who objected to the drama canceled their season subscriptions with the Guild.

In an effort to placate the subscribers, the Guild quickly sent a letter to its members explaining that it had produced the drama because it felt that Mr. Williams was a talented young writer who had received a Rockefeller Foundation grant in playwriting. The letter also predicted that his next play might well reveal his talent and be a phenomenal success. In spite of extensive rewriting during

---

the Boston run, not only to placate the censor but also to make the play more palatable for audiences, the Guild decided to close the production rather than bring it into New York. Tennessee Williams's next play, *The Glass Menagerie*, which won the Critics Circle Award, was presented by another producer. Williams later rewrote *Battle of the Angels* and retitled it *Orpheus Descending*. (The play was later filmed under still another title, *The Fugitive Kind.*) In *A History of the Pulitzer Prize Plays*, John L. Toohey commented that "it would have been better for all concerned" if *Battle of the Angels* had "rested peacefully in Boston."

Pal Joey, a musical far ahead of its time because it did not have a conventional love plot, opened in 1940 with book by John O'Hara, based on his *New Yorker* stories, and music and lyrics by Richard Rodgers and Lorenz Hart. Gene Kelly, whose performance catapulted him to stardom, made Joey an unsympathetic but interesting heel who has an affair with a wealthy matron, Mrs. Simpson. When she suspects that he is looking for a new romance, she gets rid of him before he can walk out on her. Vivienne Segal, who played Mrs. Simpson, made Hart's bawdy lyrics amusing rather than offensive. The reviews were mixed. Several critics called it adult entertainment; a greater number called it distasteful or raffish. Audience reaction was also mixed. Although the musical did not run into censorship problems in the theater, one song, "Bewitched, Bothered, and Bewildered," was barred from the radio for its lyrics. For several years, the music was also kept off the air. When *Pal Joey* was revived in the 1950s, it received better reviews, even from several of the critics who had condemned it in 1940, and better response from audiences. When it was revived still later at the New York City Center, critics called it a musical comedy classic.

The New York censors took official action in 1942 when several producers thought the old type of raffish burlesque, which had been ordered closed by the police in 1939, might be popular entertainment for wartime audiences. Michael Todd produced *Star and Garter,* a revue with Bobby Clark and former stripteaser Gypsy Rose Lee heading the cast. He incorporated the slapstick routines, the bawdy songs, and the stripteasers that had been part of the burlesque format, but he disguised the burlesque material by using elaborate settings, striking costumes, and beautiful stately showgirls whom he selected for beauty rather than talent. Several of the production numbers were as opulent as those Ziegfeld had presented in the *Follies*. Critics, commenting on the lavish production, credited Todd with bringing burlesque back to Broadway at more than double the admission charged on Forty-second Street in the 1930s.

The success of *Star and Garter* prompted the Shuberts to produce a revival of *Wine, Women, and Song* that featured Jimmy Savo and Margie Hart, a former burlesque stripteaser. Unlike *Star and Garter*, the Shubert production emphasized the vulgarity and rowdy entertainment that had caused Mayor La Guardia to bar burlesque in New York. The police ordered *Wine, Women*, and *Song*, which critics called the rawest show they had seen in years, to be closed, but the Shuberts managed to get a temporary injunction that delayed court action. The show continued on a schedule of sixteen performances a week until the police officially stopped the production after the one hundred fiftieth performance, invoked the Wales Padlock Law, and closed the Ambassador Theater where *Wine, Women*, and *Song* had been running.

The New York Drama Critics Circle had been reactivated after members accused the Pulitzer Board of censorship in bypassing *The Children's Hour*, but in the 1942–1943 season, the Critics Circle became involved in the same type of censorship. Thornton Wilder's *The Skin of Our Teeth*, which won the Pulitzer Prize, depicted the indestructibility of man through the ages, but Wilder deliberately used anachronisms to detract from the theme by making the play appear to be an out-and-out farce. The play, which opened in November, 1942, received mixed reviews. It was called "the greatest comedy of the year" as well as "the worst play ever written." Some theatergoers enjoyed the story of Mr. and Mrs. Antrobus who represented the human race from the Ice Age to the present; others left at the end of the first act.

The play starts with Mr. and Mrs. George Antrobus, their children Gladys and Henry (who symbolizes Cain), and their maid, Lily Sabina, the eternal temptress, fighting to survive the Ice Age. In the second act, Mr. Antrobus has a brief love affair with Lily Sabina, but their romance is stopped by a flood that will presumably destroy all mankind except the Antrobuses and Lily Sabina who are safe on an ark. In the third act, set in modern times after a war, the world is in ruins, but Mr. Antrobus says the human race has escaped many disasters by the skin of its teeth, and that mankind must go on hoping and living. Fredric March, Florence Eldridge, and Florence Reed received excellent notices, but Tallulah Bankhead, who played Lily Sabina, won the most glowing reviews, for she dazzled critics and audiences regardless of whether she was bandying words with Mrs. Antrobus, seducing Mr. Antrobus, or portraying a temperamental actress who stepped out of character to tell the audience she hated the play, did not understand a word of it, and refused to continue in scenes she did not like.

After the Pulitzer award was announced, Henry Morton Robinson, an editor of *Reader's Digest,* and Professor James Campbell of Sarah Lawrence College sent a letter of protest to the Pulitzer Committee claiming that Wilder had used material from *Finnegans Wake* by James Joyce without acknowledging his source. They also published two articles in the *Saturday Review of Literature* in which they cited references in Wilder's play that were similar to those in Joyce's work. Wilder, an authority on Joyce, did not respond publicly, but privately he explained to several commentators that much of Joyce's material which Robinson and Campbell had cited was based on universal ideas and could be traced to earlier literary sources. Before the Pulitzer Prize was announced, the Critics Circle had also considered making its annual award to *The Skin of Our Teeth*, but some of the drama critics, who were puzzled by the accusations made against Wilder, admitted that they did not know whether the charge of using unacknowledged material was true or false. They decided, therefore, just as the Pulitzer Committee had decided against *The Children's Hour,* to bypass Wilder's controversial *The Skin of Our Teeth,* even though many of the members agreed that it was a significant drama, and awarded their prize for the 1942–1943 season to Sidney Kingsley's *The Patriots.*

A Bell for Adano, adapted by Paul Osborn from John Hersey's novel, dealt with the postwar period and showed that invaded European countries would have to be handled with tact to convince the conquered people that America's participation in World War II was to uphold the principles of democracy. Before the play opened, rumors circulated that it included an incident, based on fact, about a short-tempered general who went into a rage during an invasion. In the first draft, Osborn had dramatized a scene in which the general alienated the people of Adano by refusing to allow mule carts to be brought back to the town even though the carts were essential for the reconstruction program. The story was discounted after the premiere in December, 1944, because Osborn had taken the short-tempered officer out of the play and had used a narrator to tell the episode of the temper tantrum.

The rumor that not only had the episode been true but also that the government preferred to have it eliminated or played down was revived later in the season. A command performance of *A Bell for Adano* scheduled to be given in Washington in honor of the President's Birthday Ball was canceled, and *Dear Ruth,* a wartime farce that had no controversial implications, was substituted. To kill any speculation about censorship, the government issued a statement explaining that *A Bell for Adano* involved too many technical problems to be moved to the capital for only one performance.

Trio by Dorothy and Howard Baker, adapted from Dorothy Baker's novel dealing with lesbianism, also opened in December,

1944. The plot involved Ray MacKenzie who realizes the dangers
involved in Janet Logan's friendship with Pauline Maury, a lesbian.
When Ray breaks up the friendship by marrying Janet, Pauline commits suicide. *Trio* had originally been booked into a New York theater owned by the Shuberts, but when it ran into a conflict with the
censors during the Philadelphia tryout and was forced to close, the
Shuberts canceled the booking for the New York theater. In spite
of arguments from Lee Sabinson, the producer of *Trio*, Lee Shubert,
who had already been ordered to close one theater, said he would
not run the risk of having the Wales Padlock Law invoked on another
of his theaters. Other theater owners also refused to book *Trio*, and
Lee Sabinson tried to get Paul Moss, New York Commissioner of
Licenses, to see the play and decide whether it would be acceptable in
New York. Moss, who refused, said he handled licenses but was not a
censor. Lee Sabinson finally leased the Belasco Theater. As soon as
Trio opened, however, church groups and vice crusaders agitated
to have the play closed. Drama critic Wolcott Gibbs, in discussing
the arguments raised against *Trio*, commented that only one of sixteen clergymen who had signed one of the protests had actually seen
the play. Pressure was exerted on public officials, and most of the
protests were sent to Commissioner Paul Moss who, acting on the
complaints, notified the owners of the Belasco Theater that he would
not renew the theater's license unless the play was evicted. Lee
Sabinson took the case to court, but the judge upheld the commissioner's order, and *Trio* was forced to close after its sixty-seventh
performance.

From 1945 to 1950, several protests were lodged with the New
York Commissioner of Licenses accusing theater box office managers
of working in collusion with speculators to sell tickets for hit shows
at far more than the specified legal fee for ticket agencies. Periodically there were reports that these complaints would be investigated,
but no action was taken.

When *South Pacific*, the Richard Rodgers–Oscar Hammerstein II musical starring Ezio Pinza and Mary Martin, tried out in Boston, speculators were being offered $50 a ticket a few days after the opening. New York advance orders were over $300,000 before the premiere on April 7, 1949, and built steadily to $500,000. Before the end of June, a ticket scandal broke in New York, for reports circulated that seats for *South Pacific*, the "hottest tickets" in years, were being sold under-the-counter at exorbitant fees. City Commissioner John M. Murtagh made several statements to newspapers about the possibility of not renewing the license for the Majestic Theater where *South Pacific* was playing, but such action was never taken, and tickets continued to sell at premiums. In spite of the long run of 1,925 performances on Broadway, *South Pacific* made even more money on the road. In Chicago, it grossed over $1,790,000 in twenty-three weeks; in Cleveland, it established a record when the theater returned over $500,000 in mail orders that could not be filled.

Although critics wrote superlative reviews for *South Pacific*—the Pulitzer Board awarded it the Pulitzer Prize for drama in 1949, the New York Drama Critics named it the best musical of the year, and record-breaking audiences all over the country crowded theaters to see the musical—there was, nevertheless, a group of protestors who objected to the song "Carefully Taught," calling it a form of propaganda. Moreover, two legislators from Georgia made a public statement expressing their disapproval of the number. In a newspaper interview, Oscar Hammerstein II said his lyrics were not propaganda but they definitely were a protest against racial prejudice. The lyrics were also an integral part of the plot because they expressed Lieutenant Cable's efforts to explain racial prejudice to Liat, the Tonkinese girl with whom he had fallen in love but whom he could not marry because she was of a different race.

9

The 1950s

In THE 1950s, reformers sporadically protested in favor of censorship, but at times officials in several cities took action even before the protests were made. In 1950, Michael Todd produced his second opulent burlesque revue, *Michael Todd's Peep Show*, which featured a cast of former burlesque comedians. Although *Peep Show* resembled Todd's *Star and Garter* as an elegantly staged burlesque show, it exceeded the earlier production in its emphasis upon raw humor and beautiful nudes. After the first night's performance, New York's Commissioner of Licenses had a conference with Michael Todd and asked for specific changes. Todd agreed to tone down the sketches and striptease routines, cut several of the bawdy burlesque gags, and make the costumes less revealing.

In January, 1952, a successful revival of Eugene O'Neill's *Desire Under the Elms* opened in New York featuring Carol Stone, Karl Malden, and Douglas Watson. Later that same season, the Brattle Theater of Cambridge gave the first production of the O'Neill drama in the Boston area. During the 1920s, when the drama had run into censorship problems in New York, the producers had decided not to attempt to book the play in Massachusetts because officials in Boston not only had made demands for extensive cuts but also had threatened to ban the play. Before presenting *Desire Under the Elms* in 1952, the Brattle Theater took precautions by checking with the authorities in Cambridge. The two policewomen who attended the opening performance, instead of asking for major changes, surprised the Brattle Theater by recommending only a few minor revisions.

A revival of Lillian Hellman's *The Children's Hour* with Kim Hunter and Patricia Neal also opened in New York in 1952 to excellent reviews but drew only moderately well and closed without recovering its investment costs. Kermit Bloomgarden, the producer, hoping to recoup his losses, decided to send the revival on the road. He was notified, however, that "it would not be judicious" to try to book the play in Boston, for the revival would still be banned in that area of Massachusetts. Bloomgarden had no difficulty booking the revival in Chicago, even though the original production had been banned there, for the Chicago censor did not oppose *The Children's Hour* or demand revisions. Unfortunately, the advance ticket sale was unsatisfactory. Although box office receipts began to improve after the opening, the reserve funds for the production were all spent, and *The Children's Hour* was forced to close before it could build up a following through word-of-mouth advertising.

An implied but unexpressed type of censorship may have affected Arthur Miller's controversial drama *The Crucible*, produced in 1953 at the time Senator Joseph McCarthy had gained power through his investigations to expose communists in the United States. In *The Crucible*, people in Salem are convicted of witchcraft by the testimony of a trollop who has lied. John Proctor is promised his freedom if he will confess and, by doing so, condemn people whom the inquisitor has on his list. Rather than send innocent victims to their death, Proctor refuses to comply with the fanatical inquisitor and is hanged. Miller, who had done extensive research on the Salem witchcraft trials of 1692, showed the strong parallel between the tactics of the inquisitors, who tortured people to confess, and the methods used in the 1950s by McCarthy in his red-baiting trials.

Rumors circulated that the Pulitzer Committee thought the anti-McCarthy implications in *The Crucible* were too controversial for a prize play and selected *Picnic* by William Inge as the Pulitzer Prize drama for 1952–1953. There were few protests over the choice, for *Picnic* also won the Critics Circle Award. *The Crucible* closed after 197 performances, a financial failure. Howard Taubman, in discussing the unsuccessful run of *The Crucible*, wondered if theatergoers could have been intimidated by McCarthy and the headline publicity given the McCarthy trials and therefore hesitated to support the drama. The reviewers may also have been overly cautious, for they commended the play but not with sufficient enthusiasm to stimulate audience interest. In the post-McCarthy era, however, critics called *The Crucible* a significant American drama when it was successfully revived off Broadway in the 1957–1958 season.

The Commissioner of Licenses was not the only city official in New York who had the power to padlock theaters. The Fire Commissioner also had the authority to close any theater that did not meet regulations specified by the fire department. Virtually all of the theaters in the Broadway sector cooperated with officials in enforcing the "no smoking" rule or in limiting standees to the rear of the auditorium. In the 1950s, however, the fire inspectors became wary of the increasing number of playhouses opening off Broadway in converted motion picture houses, old buildings, and small auditoriums. The number of these theaters increased rapidly, for producers discovered that the cost of presenting an off Broadway production, even with professional actors, would be much lower than the investment needed for an average Broadway attraction. Moreover, off Broadway theaters could operate profitably at fifty per cent of seating capacity.

One of the first prominent off Broadway theaters, The Circle in the Square, was organized by Jose Quintero, a young director, and

Theodore Mann, an attorney, who took over a former nightclub in Sheridan Square. They converted the dance floor into a three-sided arena theater, using a small rectangular area for the stage with the audience seated on the sides and at the far end. The first few productions were moderately interesting, but a revival of *Summer and Smoke* by Tennessee Williams in April, 1952, developed into a financial success that ran 257 performances, made Geraldine Page a star, and brought prominence to the off Broadway movement. In 1954, The Circle in the Square attracted further attention with *The Girl on the Via Flaminia*, adapted by Alfred Hayes from his novel about a lonely American soldier and an Italian girl who has an affair with him because hunger has driven her to prostitution. The drama drew large audiences and loomed as a potential hit for forty-three performances until the Fire Commissioner condemned The Circle in the Square as unsafe and closed the theater. Quintero and Mann later opened a new Circle in the Square that met the requirements of the Fire Commissioner.

Another off Broadway playhouse, the Theatre de Lys, formerly the Hudson Theater on Christopher Street, opened in 1952. It became evident in 1954 that the censors in New York were becoming more permissive when the Theatre de Lys produced a revival of *Maya*, which had been banned in 1928 but now was permitted to run without interference from the censors. By way of contrast, the play, which had been banned earlier in England, was not licensed in London until the late 1950s, several years after it was presented at the Theatre de Lys.

The *New York Times*, which had censored a newspaper advertisement in the 1920s for *The Demi-Virgin*, censored another theatrical advertisement in 1954 for *The Reclining Figure*, a play by Howard Kurnitz satirizing cut-throat competition in the art world. Al Hirschfeld had drawn a reclining nude, which the producers used to advertise the play, but the *Times* refused to print the picture unless the lady were more fully clothed. Hirschfeld added a brassiere to the lady's attire and the *Times* ran the revised advertisement. Other news media picked up the story, printed both pictures showing the lady with and without the brassiere, and gave *The Reclining Figure* unexpected extra publicity.

Fanny, a musical comedy by S. N. Behrman and Joshua Logan with songs by Harold Rome, was based on a trilogy by Marcel Pagnol. The musical opened in 1954 starring Ezio Pinza and Walter Slezak. The cast, however, included Nejla Ates, an exotic belly dancer who appeared in the production for less than five minutes but drew more publicity than the stars for her specialty number in which she wore a minimal costume while she gyrated. A life-size photograph of Miss Ates displayed in front of the theater became a topic of conversation for theatergoers and a frequent item for newspaper columnists. As the musical continued its run, Miss Ates began cutting her abbreviated costume even more by discarding a well-placed bead or two until the police notified producer David Merrick that Miss Ates was to wear the original costume or the show would be closed. On the other hand, no official action was taken against Sidney Kingsley's *Lunatics and Lovers*, a comedy produced that same season, which included a scene showing Sheila Bond taking a bubble bath on stage.

Cat on a Hot Tin Roof by Tennessee Williams, which won both the Critics Circle Award and the Pulitzer Prize for the 1954–1955 season, discussed perversion, greed, and homosexuality in lusty dialogue. The principal characters included Big Daddy, who does not know that he is dying of cancer; Brick, his son, who has become an alcoholic because he repressed his homosexual attraction to his friend Skipper and drove Skipper to suicide; and Maggie, Brick's frustrated wife, who knows that unless she has a child, Big Daddy will leave his estate to his son George. In the last act, Maggie lies to Big Daddy telling him she is pregnant, and then pleads with Brick to make the lie come true. The printed text had two third acts—

Williams's original draft in which Big Daddy is kept off stage; and a new third act that Elia Kazan, the director, made Williams write to bring Big Daddy back on stage for an effective climax.

The Pulitzer Prize award to *Cat on a Hot Tin Roof* surprised a great many people who remembered that the Board had bypassed *What Price Glory?* for language that was far less earthy than the dialogue in *Cat on a Hot Tin Roof*. The jurors for the award were reported to have recommended *The Flowering Peach* by Clifford Odets, but the Advisory Board overruled the selection and named *Cat on a Hot Tin Roof* as the prize-winning play.

When *Cat on a Hot Tin Roof* opened in New York, several critics commented on the language in their reviews. Jack Gaver, critic for the United Press, said the rough dialogue "could be eliminated for the most part without altering the story an iota or without destroying the realism that the author probably fancies he has obtained by using it." John Chapman, critic for the *Daily News*, felt that "the considerable amount of dirty talk in it was mere boyish bravado and rather pointless." Two weeks after the New York opening, Edward T. McCaffrey, Commissioner of Licenses, who had received several complaints, took specific action on a complaint made by the Children's Aid Society. He saw the play and after the performance had a conference backstage. Although he was assured that the children in the cast were in their dressing rooms during the scenes in which the objectionable passages of dialogue were spoken on stage, McCaffrey, nevertheless, asked for revisions in several sequences and specified that one obscene joke, which was irrelevant to the action, be cut. These changes were made and *Cat on a Hot Tin Roof* continued its successful run in New York for 694 performances. The road company, however, was not as successful, particularly in Chicago where the critics objected to the replacements for the original Broadway cast.

In London, *Cat on a Hot Tin Roof* failed to duplicate its success in New York. It also had more problems with censors in Britain than it had in the United States. Since the subject of homosexuality was still taboo in England, the Lord Chamberlain refused to license the drama for public performances. It was produced, therefore, at a club theater with performances for members only. *Cat on a Hot Tin Roof*, however, did not please the English critics because the producers, instead of presenting the New York version, used Williams's original but less effective third act, which could not sustain audience interest because Big Daddy, the most vigorous character in the play, was kept off stage.

Eugene O'Neill completed his autobiographical play *Long Day's Journey Into Night* in the early 1940s and gave Bennett Cerf, at Random House, a sealed manuscript that was not to be opened until twenty-five years after O'Neill's death or until twenty years after all the characters involved in the play had died. In 1955, two years after O'Neill died, Bennett Cerf refused to comply with Mrs. O'Neill's request that he break his agreement with O'Neill and publish the work before the specified date. Since O'Neill's will stipulated that his wife had full control of his plays, Mrs. O'Neill took the manuscript from Random House and had it published by the Yale University Press, and gave the Royal Dramatic Theater in Stockholm permission to produce the tragedy in 1956.

When *Long Day's Journey Into Night* opened in New York in 1956, it towered over all other plays of the season and won both the Critics Circle Award and the Pulitzer Prize as the best play of the year. Only minor objections were raised to the repetitive speeches and unorthodox length, for the play ran approximately four hours with performances starting at 7:30 P.M. There was no definite plot development; instead, the drama presented a deep, introspective view of each of the four principals. Moreover, O'Neill did not soften the characterizations of himself, his father, mother, and brother, or gloss over the unpleasantness in their family life. The play reveals that the father, called Mr. Tyrone, is a miser who no longer has any illusions about his acting career. Mrs. Tyrone is a drug addict because her husband called in a quack doctor who gave her morphine when she was ailing after her second son, Edmund (Eugene), was born. Mr. Tyrone, knowing that Edmund has consumption, is ready to send him to a cheap institution. The older son, James, is an alcoholic who is jealous of his brother's talent. As the play ends, the three men are drunk, and Mrs. Tyrone, high on drugs, is in a world of illusion.

The drama had no problems with censorship in New York, but in 1962, Abner McCall, president of Baylor University, a Baptist school in Texas, ordered the University Theater's production of *Long Day's Journey Into Night* to close after its fourth performance because it was "not in keeping with the University ideals." McCall admitted that a delegation of ministers had demanded that he close the production, but he added that he had also received numerous protests against the blasphemous dialogue. Since the protestors insisted that the drama ridiculed the Christian religion, he banned the play because he did not think it was "in good taste for a church-related university to produce." Other university spokesmen said the trouble might have been averted if the script could have been revised, but the contract with Mrs. O'Neill specified that the drama could not be changed or cut.

Paul Baker, chairman of the drama department at Baylor, admitted that the drama had strong language. He insisted, however, that it was one of the greatest plays of its time and that people from all parts of Texas, including high school teachers who wanted to bring their best pupils with them, had planned to see Baylor's production. The local papers sided with Baker by denouncing the school's censorship. In his widely read newspaper column, drama critic Gynter Quinn said that Baylor had practiced such censorship before by refusing to let the drama department produce *Mister Roberts*, and that it had forced the department to revise and cut lines in the Pulitzer Prize musical comedy *Of Thee I Sing*. As a result of the dispute over *Long Day's Journey Into Night,* Paul Baker, eleven members of the drama department, and Mrs. Baker resigned from their positions at Baylor. Almost immediately, Trinity College, a Presbyterian school in San Antonio, Texas, announced that Paul Baker would become the new head of their drama department.

A censorship case in England in the early 1900s was paralleled by a case in New York in the late 1950s. In England, the Lord Chamberlain had suddenly revoked the license for *Secrets of the Harem*, a play that had been touring for several years. In response to protests from producers who had a large investment in costumes and scenery, and from actors who were thrown out of work, an unofficial explanation was given stating that a member of the Turkish Embassy objected to the play, which he thought was in poor taste. After a parliamentary committee began to investigate the ban, the Lord Chamberlain agreed to license the play if the word *Harem* were omitted from the title. The play was then advertised as *Secrets* —— ——. The revised title soon became far more suggestive than the original because the blanks on posters and billboards provided ample space for pranksters to write in back-yard-fence obscenities. In New York, the same type of censorship was imposed during the 1958– 1959 season on an off Broadway revival of John Ford's seventeenth-century drama *'Tis Pity She's a Whore*. The city officials did not interfere with the play itself, but they ordered the management to omit the final word from the title on posters and billboards outside the theater. The *New York Times* also acted as censor by refusing to print any advertisements for the play unless the same word was cut. Once again the blank space attracted attention and made the censored title far more salacious than the original.

As late as the 1950s, American dramatists were cautious in representing recent United States presidents or their families on stage, not only out of respect for the people involved but also because any unfavorable representation could result in libel suits such as those filed against *Masque of Kings*. This caution may possibly have reflected the attitude of the English censor, for the ban on representing members of the Royal Family on stage was not lifted until all censorship in England was abolished. In 1951, the Lord

Chamberlain had banned an operetta that dealt with Queen Victoria and Prince Albert because the libretto was historically inaccurate and because the Queen sang on stage. This ban came as a surprise, for in 1949 the Lord Chamberlain had licensed *The Glorious Days*, a musical in which Anna Neagle, as Queen Victoria, not only sang "Drink To Me Only With Thine Eyes" but also taught Prince Albert to dance. Miss Neagle, however, had played an ambulance driver who was injured and, while suffering from a concussion, only dreamed that she was the Queen. The Lord Chamberlain, therefore, had licensed the musical because he felt that she was not actually impersonating the Queen on stage. On the other hand, the Lord Chamberlain refused to license sketches involving Prince Charles, the love affairs of Edward VII, the recorded voice of King George V in a documentary drama, and a reference to King George VI's statement that he did not want to be king. The censor also banned a sketch dealing with the sinking of a royal barge and then showing the Queen swimming to shore, even though the sketch had been presented on television in the David Frost program "That Was the Week That Was."

Two American productions in the 1950s demonstrated different methods of presenting American presidents or prominent political figures on stage without offending the people involved or their relatives. In 1950, when the musical *Call Me Madam*, with songs by Irving Berlin and book by Howard Lindsay and Russel Crouse, opened in New York, Ethel Merman starred as Mrs. Sally Adams, a famous Washington hostess whom President Truman sends as an ambassadress to a mythical country, Lichtenburg. Lindsay and Crouse denied that the characterization of Mrs. Adams had any connection with Perle Mesta, whom President Truman had sent to Luxembourg. Even the critics agreed that the ambassadress lampooned Mrs. Mesta's position but not Mrs. Mesta herself, for Sally Adams was actually a composite of the popular heroines Merman had played—the brash, good-hearted woman who wins over the opposition. Moreover, Mrs.

Mesta, who was pleased with the musical and with the characterization of Mrs. Sally Adams, appeared on a television program that featured songs from *Call Me Madam*. There was no denying, however,
the direct references to the Truman family. Some of the most amusing sequences were Ethel Merman's phone conversations with
Truman that began, "Hello, Harry," and the finale, when an actor
impersonating Truman appeared on stage. The musical even included the song "They Like Ike," which later became Eisenhower's
campaign song. There was little if any adverse criticism of the political implications of the musical because the references to Mrs. Mesta,
Dwight Eisenhower, and the Trumans were witty, in good taste,
and actually very complimentary.

Dore Schary, on the other hand, dealt with far more controversial
material when he wrote *Sunrise at Campobello*, the biographical
drama of Franklin Delano Roosevelt's struggle to conquer polio.
Schary made no effort to disguise the members of the Roosevelt
family, Governor Alfred Smith, or other political figures involved
in Roosevelt's political career by changing names. The play also included Roosevelt's quarrel with his mother over his decision to
return to politics when she felt he should retire to Hyde Park. She
also disapproved of his friendship with Louis Howe who was en-
couraging Roosevelt to resume his career. Roosevelt, the only man
to be elected to the presidency four times, had to be characterized
with discretion to avoid antagonizing his millions of admirers.
Schary faced the same problem in portraying Eleanor Roosevelt,
for she had become one of the most admired women in American
history. Schary, nevertheless, succeeded in revealing the pressures she
was forced to bear during her husband's convalescence as well as
her efforts to reunite Roosevelt and his mother after their quarrel.

Schary avoided possible litigation or dissatisfaction by discussing
the play and the characterizations with members of the Roosevelt
family, who cooperated with him to make certain that the drama
would not embarrass any of the people represented in the play. The

final draft spanned the period from August 10, 1921, the day Roosevelt was stricken with polio, to the night he nominated Al Smith for the presidency of the United States at the Democratic National Convention in New York City. In the final short but effective scene, Roosevelt takes ten steps to the podium. The crowd yells; the band plays "The Sidewalks of New York"; and Roosevelt, holding the lectern, smiles and waves his right hand, a gesture that people would always associate with him, as the curtains close. When the play opened in 1958, it owed much of its success to Ralph Bellamy who gave an amazing performance as Roosevelt, for he not only captured the famous grin and magnetic voice but also depicted Roosevelt's strength and desperation in trying to conquer his physical weakness.

In the late 1950s, rumors circulated that the federal government had censored productions selected to represent the United States at the World's Fair held in Brussels. *West Side Story*, a musical by Arthur Laurents with music by Leonard Bernstein and lyrics by Stephen Sondheim, was included in the first list of musicals under consideration for the Fair, but when the final selections were announced, *West Side Story* had been dropped and replaced by another Bernstein musical, *Wonderful Town*, based on the successful comedy *My Sister Eileen.* Although there was no official explanation given, it was assumed that the government felt *West Side Story* would give Europeans a distorted picture of American life, for the plot involved gang fights and violence, and the choreography by Jerome Robbins included crouching, finger-snapping dancers wielding ominous switchblades in routines that emphasized the animalism, brutality, and hatred of the gang members. The cancellation may also have been prompted by the reviews when *West Side Story* first opened in 1957. Several critics thought the violence and ill-fated love story were not appropriate for the musical theater. Even Leonard Bernstein's score did not win unanimous approval. When *West Side Story* was brought back to Broadway in 1960, however, critics hailed it as a masterpiece; the gang warfare, which had seemed exaggerated in 1957, now represented an authentic portrait of the conflicting rebel groups in New York; and Bernstein's score, enhanced by Sondheim's lyrics, was now acclaimed for its melodies, its intricate orchestrations, and its difficult arrangements, which required highly trained singers.

John Osborne's *The Entertainer* was censored both in London and in New York although the changes ordered in the two cities were not the same. The drama starred Laurence Olivier as Archie Rice, a cheap vaudeville actor who has little talent and abuses people to cover up for his shortcomings. The play alternated vaudeville skits with scenes about Archie's family life. Before the Lord Chamberlain licensed *The Entertainer* in 1957, he ordered an extensive list of changes in the dialogue, particularly those speeches that included vulgarities, obscenities, or earthy expressions. He also demanded that several lines mocking religious practices or lines quoted from religious writings be deleted. When the play opened in New York in 1958, members of the Commissioner of Licensing's department apparently asked for no changes in the dialogue. They did, however, object to the seminude actress, Jeri Archer, who appeared on stage as "Brittannia" during Archie's act. Brittannia, who wore only a wisp of mesh above the waist, dropped the mesh and remained topless for the rest of the scene. In response to an order from the New York censors, the scene was changed and Brittannia no longer dropped the mesh.

10

The 1960s

During the 1950s and early 1960s, theater columnists sporadically referred to the fact that very few plays that were licensed in England were heavily censored in New York. In other American cities, however, local censors were more active. The Massachusetts Civil Liberties Union protested whenever Richard J. Sinnott, the city censor in Boston—who held the appointive office of chief of the licensing bureau—demanded cuts and changes. In 1960, Mr. Sinnott objected to *Lock Up Your Daughters*, a musical that had been a hit in London, and ordered extensive revisions with at least one scene deleted. Instead of opposing Sinnott, producer Daniel Crawford tried to make the changes. The show was not running smoothly and Crawford realized that it needed to be completely rewritten. He therefore decided to close the musical prematurely after one week rather than take a chance by bringing it into New York. Although Crawford explained that censorship had nothing to do with the closing, the Civil Liberties Union took up the fight against Sinnott's censorship. The CLU was unsuccessful, however, for Arthur G. Coffey, the attorney who defended Sinnott, verified the fact that Sinnott was acting within his rights and had the legal authority to censor *Lock Up Your Daughters.*

Even plays that were banned or heavily censored in England, such as those dealing with homosexuals, had little or no opposition in New York. *A Taste of Honey,* by a nineteen-year-old playwright, Shelagh Delaney, produced in 1960, dealt with Josephine, an illegitimate, lonely girl who has an affair with a black sailor. He leaves her, not knowing that she is pregnant, and a homosexual looks after her until her mother, who is obviously a trollop, arrives. In London, *A Taste of Honey* was presented at a club theater because the Lord Chamberlain banned it for public performances; in New York, the Critics Circle named it as the best foreign play of the year.

There were attempts in 1960 and 1961 to push through a bill in Congress to create a commission on "Noxious and Obscene Matters and Materials." The aim of the bill was to check on obscenity in drama, motion pictures, and publications as well as to stop the increased circulation of hard-core pornography. The bill also proposed that the commission include clergymen, school officials, a state attorney general, prosecutors, representatives from government agencies, and at least one United States senator. The first attempt to pass the bill was killed in the House of Representatives; in a second attempt, the bill was blocked in the Senate.

By 1961, records revealed that the Special Services Division of the United States Army in Europe had censored, cut, or rewritten Broadway plays "to keep them clean," and that the cuts or revisions had generally been made without informing the authors or the Dramatists Guild. The Special Services Division admitted that "four letter words, double meanings, and immoral situations were cleaned up" before plays were produced, but the revisions were made to give the military forces "pure entertainment." A production of *Mister Roberts* had been banned in Heidelberg in 1950 because the language was "too salty." *The Moon Is Blue,* which involved an attractive young girl who constantly bragged about her virginity, was also banned at several military installations. The Special Services Division explained that military base commanders had the power to ban productions but usually followed recommendations made by base chaplains, who were asked to suggest what type of play should be produced. The Special Services Division, however, did not offer any explanation for some of the absurd changes. When the Seventh Army Entertainment Branch produced *Hellzapoppin'*, for example, the title had been changed to *Hecksapoppin'*.

Army officials generally selected the production for the United States military-sponsored theater in Frankfurt, Germany. The playhouse was organized to improve German-American relations, and the cast and crew were composed of both American and German military personnel, in order to give Germans a chance to work with Americans on American plays. Both German and American civilians were invited to see the plays, but no one could appear in the productions unless he was connected with the military installation. *Stalag 17*, a play dealing with American military prisoners in Germany, was not permitted to be produced at the Frankfurt theater because army officials thought it would hinder efforts to improve German-American relations in the postwar period. Oddly enough, *Stalag 17* was produced professionally in the German theaters.

Military officials denied that all plays by Tennessee Williams, with the exception of *The Glass Menagerie*, had been banned for Army productions. They had not granted permission for *A Streetcar Named Desire* to be produced at the theater in Frankfurt, but they did offer statistics on the number of Williams plays produced in all the military installations in Europe: *Portrait of a Madonna* had been given for five performances; *The Glass Menagerie* had been given for fifty-seven performances in twelve different productions; and *A Streetcar Named Desire* had been given for at least one performance.

Censorship in Massachusetts again came under fire in 1962. Plans had been made to present *The Zoo Story* by Edward Albee and *Call*

Me By My Rightful Name by Michael Shurtleff in the high-school auditorium in Rockport, Massachusetts. *The Zoo Story*, which brought national recognition to Edward Albee, was first produced off Broadway in 1960. The play was set in Central Park and dealt with a beatnik who annoys a man to make him aware of the seething world around him. The ending is violent, for the beatnik is killed. *Call Me By My Rightful Name,* suggested by the novel *The Whipping Boy* by S. F. Pfoutz, was produced off Broadway in 1961. The three principal characters are a young white man, the white girl whom he loves, and his roommate, a black man. When the young man discovers that his girl and his roommate have had an affair, he becomes violent. The play ends in confusion, for Shurtleff does not resolve the problems nor does he clarify his characterizations.

Rockport's Board of Selectmen, who refused to allow the plays to be produced because they dealt with sex and violence, also objected to the realistic dialogue, the homosexual overtones in *The Zoo Story,* and the racial triangle in *Call Me By My Rightful Name.* After protests were made against the banning, the Board of Selectmen gave permission for *The Zoo Story* to be produced but refused to lift the ban on *Call Me By My Rightful Name.* Because of the controversy, the Board decided that in the future they would not stop plays from being presented, but they warned producers that they would still cancel any play after the opening performance if they felt that it was not "in good taste."

Petitions for legislation to censor the theater in the state of New York were circulated periodically. Several members of the New York Legislature, in response to strong protests from such ethnic groups as the Italians and the Poles, who objected to racial stereotyping, discussed proposing a bill to stop "group slander," but no definite plans were made to present such a law for adoption.

Joseph Papp's New York Shakespeare Festival, subsidized by the City of New York, ran into difficulties in 1962 when Papp opened the summer season at the new Central Park Delacorte

Theater with *The Merchant of Venice* starring George C. Scott as Shylock. Religious leaders of several faiths vigorously protested against the use of public funds to produce an anti-Semitic play, but their objections were offset by excellent reviews, which city officials felt counterbalanced the protests.

Reports of unofficial censorship circulated when *Mr. President,* a musical comedy by Howard Lindsay and Russel Crouse with songs by Irving Berlin, opened in Boston in 1962. The libretto dealt with a fictional president, his wife and family, their life in the White House, and their return to civilian life. Advance newspaper publicity intimated that the musical could be linked to John F. Kennedy and his family, but after the opening, critics suggested that the authors had apparently been asked to cut parts of the script that might offend presidential families, particularly the Kennedys. *Mr. President* may originally have started as a lampoon similar to the earlier Berlin–Lindsay–Crouse musical *Call Me Madam,* but by the time *Mr. President* reached New York, direct references to a specific president or his family had been cut, the president and first lady were fictional characters, and what may have been intended as an amusing satire emerged as a routine musical that failed.

Coincidentally, attempts to satirize the Kennedys were officially censored in London that same year. Before *The Premise,* an American revue, opened in London in 1962, the Lord Chamberlain ordered the producers to delete a sketch about President John Kennedy and his family in which Caroline Kennedy, the daughter, was portrayed as the brains in the White House. Although the producers had received a cable from President Kennedy stating that he had no objections to the sketch, the Lord Chamberlain banned it. That same year, when a revue, *See You Inside,* opened in Liverpool, the Lord Chamberlain ordered the producers to cut a sketch in which Moira Lister satirized Jacqueline Kennedy.

In the 1962–1963 season, *Who's Afraid of Virginia Woolf?*

by Edward Albee won the Critics Circle Award as the best play of the year. The Pulitzer Advisory Committee also endorsed Albee's drama, but the Pulitzer Board overruled the recommendation and decided not to award any prize for drama. This decision raised the same accusations of censorship that had been made against the Pulitzer Board when it bypassed *What Price Glory?* and *The Children's Hour*. Furthermore, John Gassner and John Mason Brown, the two jurors who had recommended *Who's Afraid of Virginia Woolf?* resigned from the Advisory Committee.

Since Albee's drama ran three hours, there had been reports that the script would be cut, but after the enthusiastic reviews helped *Who's Afraid of Virginia Woolf?* become the first sell-out of the season, no changes were made. Albee created strongly developed characterizations whose lusty dialogue shocked some audiences; others called the play an exhausting, emotional experience. The action takes place from 2:00 A.M. to dawn, and the plot, a mixture of fact and fancy, involves two couples. George, a college professor, is six years younger than Martha, his coarse, outspoken wife. Unable to have children, they have created an imaginary son whom they use as a means of baiting each other. When Nick, a younger professor, and Honey, his wife, stop in for a drink, Martha disregards George's warning and discusses their imaginary child as though he were real. Martha seduces Nick, and, in retaliation, George says he has received a telegram informing him of the death of their son. Nick and Honey realize that the child is imaginary, and George and Martha are left alone, as the play ends, to face a future of frustration.

The drama received wide publicity not only for its earthiness but also for its symbolism. Columnists, for example, asked if Albee had used the names George and Martha because George and Martha Washington had been childless. People hunting for symbolism in the title discovered that Albee had originally called the play *The Exorcism,* but after he saw *Who's Afraid of Virginia Woolf?* written on a wall, he decided to use it as a gag title. The discussions stimulated interest not only in New York, where the play had no problems with censors, but also on the road where it met strong opposition.

When *Who's Afraid of Virginia Woolf?* was scheduled to open in Boston, Richard J. Sinnott, the city censor, called the play "a cesspool" and ordered nine cuts in the dialogue, particularly in the use of the name *Jesus Christ* as an expletive. The critics snidely commented that Sinnott's definition of the Deity meant only Christ, for the word God was not ordered deleted. They also pointed out that Sinnott had ordered lines cut that had already been used in a television adaptation. Although Albee believed that plays should not be censored, he agreed to make the revisions, and producer Richard Barr and Clinton Wilder said the cuts did not seriously detract from the basic integrity of the drama. After the Boston newspapers censured Albee for complying with the censor's demands, he explained that since Sinnott had the power to revoke theater licenses, he knew that if he did not carry out Sinnott's orders, he would be responsible for closing the theater. During its first run in Boston, *Who's Afraid of Virginia Woolf?* was virtually a sell-out, but when it was scheduled for a return engagement at the end of the season, the mail orders and advance ticket sales were poor, and the booking was canceled.

Local authorities in St. Paul who canceled a showing of Albee's drama said they wanted to avoid offending the public, but the play had no interference from officials when it was produced in the adjacent twin city of Minneapolis. Newspapers periodically reported that censorship or cancellations of the play in other cities may have been caused by Albee's insistence that performances be given for nonsegregated audiences, but these reports were never substantiated. When the play was banned in South Africa, the African producers wrote to the William Morris Agency asking for a copy of the revised script that had been used in Boston so that it could be sent to the board of censors in South Africa. The agency notified the producers that there was no official copy of the Boston script but suggested that the producers might try to negotiate directly with Edward Albee by sending him a list of revisions demanded by the South African censors and asking Albee if he would comment on the deletions or changes.

In London, the Lord Chamberlain had refused to license *The Establishment*, an English revue, for public performances, and the producers therefore had presented it at a private club. When John Krimsky, Peter Cook, and Nicholas Luard produced *The Establishment* in New York at the Strollers Theater-Club, an off Broadway theater, in 1963, a great many theatergoers were offended by a sketch that involved a discussion between Christ and two thieves who were to be crucified with him. The thieves were curious to know why their companion spoke with an upper-class accent while they spoke with Cockney accents. Bernard J. O'Donnell, New York City's License Commissioner, called the sketch "a sacrilege" and "tasteless," and notified coproducer John Krimsky that the state penal code did not permit actors to represent the Deity on stage. Krimsky admitted that people had walked out on the performance. He said, however, that the skit had been intended to satirize British accents but not religion. After Krimsky was told that the commissioner had received numerous complaints and that the theater license could be revoked if he did not cooperate with O'Donnell, Krimsky agreed to drop the sketch, which lasted only ninety seconds. He also admitted to O'Donnell that he had considered dropping the sketch anyway because he had received a great many protests not only in New York but also in Chicago and in Washington.

The producers of *The Establishment*, however, managed to gain a good deal of publicity by capitalizing on the running feud in New York between David Merrick and the New York drama critics. The year before, Merrick had found seven men with the same names as the prominent New York critics and he had advertised signed, complimentary reviews presumably written by these men for his musical *Subways Are For Sleeping*. The producers of *The Establishment* tracked down a mailman in Philadelphia named David Merrick and supposedly had him write a signed comment calling *The Establishment* a better show than Merrick's productions of *Oliver* and *Stop the World—I Want to Get Off*.

The possibility of a lawsuit loomed after *A Case of Libel,* an aptly titled drama, opened in October, 1963. The play, which Henry Denker adapted from Louis Nizer's biographical book *My Life In Court,* dealt with one of Nizer's most famous cases, the successful libel suit brought by ex-war correspondent Quentin Reynolds against newspaper columnist Westbrook Pegler. Rumors began circulating that the producers of *A Case of Libel* would be sued because Denker's dramatization differed from the facts given in Nizer's book and the columnist was depicted as a ruthless opportunist. There are no confirmed reports or items in theatrical columns to indicate whether the case was ever ready to be filed or whether the controversy was settled out of court.

The contrast between censorship in London and in New York was again evident in connection with John Osborne's *Luther*, which dealt with the history of the Reformation, the reasons for Martin Luther's break with the Vatican, and the founding of the Protestant Church. There seemed little likelihood that the play would be licensed in London because Osborne refused to make cuts ordered by the Lord Chamberlain or to change any of the wording to which the Lord Chamberlain had objected. When the managers of the English Stage Company, who considered presenting the play at private club performances, discussed the changes with the Assistant Comptroller, the Lord Chamberlain reexamined the play and modified his order for revisions. The changes were made, and the play was licensed for public performances. *Luther* opened in New York in 1963 without any orders for deletions and received better reviews than it had in

London. At the end of the season, the Critics Circle, with seven votes out of eighteen, named *Luther* as the best foreign play of the year. John Osborne also won the Tony Award as author of the best drama of the season.

Strong protests were made in both London and New York, on the other hand, against *The Deputy* (called *The Representative* in London), a drama by Rolf Hochhuth and adapted by Jerome Rothenberg. Originally produced in Berlin, the play raised the question of how much the Church was to blame for the mass murder of Jews by the Nazis and just how much Pope Pius XII was to blame by remaining silent instead of attempting to prevent the Nazi atrocities. Churchmen who saw the Berlin production predicted that it would run into trouble, for it would arouse Roman Catholics, not only for its accusations against the Pope but also because Hochhuth was a Protestant. The churchmen also felt that it would start a strong anti-German movement because Hochhuth was a German. Other protestors said the play was in error—that Pope Pius XII had to remain silent in order to prevent strong reprisals and greater atrocities by the Germans; the Nazis might even have killed the Pope and then declared that he was murdered because he had tried to escape. On the other hand, by remaining silent, Pope Pius XII had been able to help a great number of refugees secretly.

When the Royal Shakespeare Company wanted to produce the play, Lord Cobbold, the Lord Chamberlain, had to take extra precautions in making his decision because the Royal Shakespeare Company was subsidized by the government. The Lord Chamberlain finally agreed to license the play but only under certain conditions. The management was to display a notice stating that children under sixteen would not be admitted because film sequences used were rated X. The Lord Chamberlain also insisted that the management publish in the theater program a rebuttal statement made by an authoritative Roman Catholic. The Company did this by publishing letters from Cardinal Montini—who later became Pope Paul VI—

and an article by the editor of the *Catholic Herald* who said the play
was incorrect and that it had been popular in Germany because it
made the Nazis feel less guilty.

When *The Representative* opened in London, the reviews were
definitely mixed. Various religious groups protested against the play;
posters outside the Aldwych Theater were defaced; and the actor who
played Eichmann on stage said he had received numerous threats
on his life. British theater managers generally agreed that if the news
media had not played up the controversy before the production went
into rehearsal, *The Representative* would never have been licensed
in England.

When Billy Rose announced that he intended to produce *The
Deputy* in New York, *Insider's Newsletter* published an article,
"Religious Storm Coming," which predicted that religious groups
would vigorously object to the drama. The Reverend Robert A.
Graham, an associate editor of *America,* a Roman Catholic weekly
published by the Society of Jesus, denounced the play, calling it
typical Nazi literature. Dale Francis, in an article published in a
Catholic newspaper, *Our Sunday Visitor,* said the play was fiction
and that Hochhuth, now aged thirty-three, was once a member of
the Nazi youth movement in Germany. Herman Shumlin, who was
scheduled to stage Billy Rose's production, denied reports that the
Habimah Players of Israel had canceled their production of *The
Deputy.* The director of Habimah, however, announced that the
Israeli production had been postponed indefinitely.

After Billy Rose decided not to produce the play, Herman Shumlin took over the production, which he also directed. Since the play
had run seven hours in its original form, Shumlin conferred with
Hochhuth who agreed to have it cut down to three hours. *The Deputy*
opened in New York in February, 1964, in spite of protests from
clergymen and threats from unidentified sources against Shumlin.
On opening night, members of the American Fascist organization,
wearing storm trooper uniforms, picketed the theater. Although most

of the drama critics thought the play was weak, *The Deputy* ran 316 performances. In the spring of 1964, Herman Shumlin received a Tony Award for presenting the drama, but the protestors were still insisting that *The Deputy* should never have been produced because it was pure fiction.

In 1964, another attempt was made to censor political drama. The Actors Studio produced a repertory of three plays, the most controversial of which was *Blues for Mister Charlie* by James Baldwin, one of the first plays to present the black militant and his point of view. The drama dealt with a Negro who has been living in the North, comes back to the South, insults the whites in his community, and is murdered by a white storekeeper. Several critics thought the play was confused propaganda; others championed it. Tom Driver wrote a favorable review for the *Reporter* in which he called Baldwin an outspoken dramatist who was not afraid to say what he thought. When the editors of the *Reporter* refused to print the review, Driver resigned. Within a very short time, the review was printed in both the *Village Voice* and *Christianity and Crisis*.

During the 1963–1964 season, federal officers closed an off Broadway theater operated by a group known as the Living Theater. The founders, Julian Beck and his wife Judith Malina, were arrested, tried, and convicted on charges of impeding federal officers who were performing their duties in closing the theater. Beck and Malina were also convicted for contempt of court. Several groups opposed to censorship, assuming that the theater had been closed by the New York Commissioner of Licenses, rushed to support Beck and Malina, but the court trial revealed that censorship had not been involved. The federal government had padlocked the theater because the Living Theater, which Beck said operated as a nonprofit group, owed more than thirty thousand dollars in back rent, admission taxes, withholding tax payments, and insurance for employees. Although Beck insisted that he might have been able to pay the bills and save his company if his theater had not been closed, he was found guilty and ordered to serve two sixty-day sentences. Judith Malina was ordered to serve two thirty-day sentences. Beck and Malina appealed the case, and while it was pending, they were given permission to take their company abroad. When they returned, they both served terms in jail.

Another court case during this period involved Lenny Bruce, a nightclub entertainer, who was arrested in 1964 for indecency and for using foul language in his performance at a Greenwich Village cafe. Bruce, who had previously been arrested on similar charges, had become known for using any type of expression involving vulgarity, obscenity, blasphemy, or perversion to shock audiences. Several performers who knew Bruce said he was amused when he scandalized people but frustrated when he went to extremes and got only impassive silence instead of a negative reaction. After his arrest in 1964, approximately one hundred prominent college professors, novelists, poets, and dramatists came to Bruce's defense and charged that his arrest violated the constitutional guarantee of free speech. Moreover, they argued that audiences and not the police department in New York or any other city should decide what was offensive. This last argument was somewhat invalid, for even Bruce admitted that in some nightclubs a number of patrons had refused to stay until he finished his act. Earl Wilson in *The Show Business Nobody Knows* reported that at one performance, a busload of 120 people walked out en masse during the act. Bruce's supporters called him brilliant and compared his satire to the works of Rabelais, Swift, and Aristophanes. At the court trial, after hearing a tape recording made by plainclothesmen, a grand jury decided that Bruce's act was obscene. A similar charge was made in Los Angeles, but the case was dismissed.

Lenny, a drama by Julian Barry with music by Tom O'Horgan, tried to portray Lenny Bruce sympathetically. The play dealt with his marriage, his obscenity trials, and his nightclub routines in which he satirized false modesty, hypocrisy, and religion. The play interested audiences not for its language, which by 1971 had lost much of its shock value, but for the remarkable performance given by Cliff Gorman who portrayed Lenny Bruce.

In the 1960s, the protests against Bruce's arrest had been aimed primarily at insuring freedom of speech. Similar protests made in the 1970s against obscenity cases were often futile, for the United States Supreme Court, after considering several of the cases, handed down a decision that permitted local governments to determine what constituted pornography, thus virtually establishing local censorship in many states.

When the University of Minnesota received a $74,000 Rockefeller Foundation grant to help young playwrights, Arthur Kopit and Terrence McNally were selected as the first recipients. Kopit's *Oh, Dad, Poor Dad, Mama's Hung You in the Closet and I'm Feelin' So Sad* had been one of the most successful plays off Broadway in the 1961–1962 season and had later been sent on tour. Before their grants expired, Kopit and McNally were dissatisfied with the way the university was handling their scripts and protested that the school was censoring their plays. A university official said that the school did not censor. Grants offering financial help, he explained, did not stipulate that plays had to be staged for public performances, the implication being that only plays that the university considered to have merit would be produced.

In the spring of 1965, Kopit and McNally both had plays produced in New York. Kopit's *The Day The Whores Came Out to Play Tennis,* which dealt with an off-stage group of boisterous women who upset an exclusive country club, opened off Broadway as part of a double bill that failed after twenty-four performances. McNally's *And Things That Go Bump in the Night* dealt with a fiendish woman and her two fiendish children who live in a bomb shelter and lure a young man into their home, torture him, and finally drive him into a state of hysteria. The play opened on Broadway in April, 1965, and received scathing reviews. Several critics quoted a line of dialogue from the play, "We will continue," in order to add the comment, "Oh, no, you won't." The drama might well have closed after the first performance, but the producers tried to force a run by charging only one dollar per ticket. Approximately seven hundred people came to see the third performance at this reduced rate, and the play drew large audiences for the rest of the week. During the second week, the producers tried going back to the regular price scale but the show drew poorly until the admission was lowered to two dollars. Box office receipts were not high enough to cover operating expenses, however, and the play closed after sixteen performances.

The charges of obscenity and foul language made against Lenny Bruce could easily have been made against a number of plays produced within the next two seasons. A double bill, *The Slave* and *The Toilet*, two one-act plays by Le Roi Jones, opened off Broadway in December, 1964. *The Slave* predicted the possibility of an armed revolution in its story of a Negro leader who comes to the home of his former wife, a white woman now married to a college professor, and threatens both of them. *The Toilet*, the more controversial of the two plays, was set in a boys' lavatory in an integrated school and concerned a group of black schoolboys who beat up a white boy because he has a homosexual attraction to their leader. Both plays were filled with brutality and with obscenities, which lost their shock value by constant repetition, but *The Toilet* was the more compassionate of the two plays, for the Negro leader comes back to comfort the white victim, although he has to sneak away from his gang to do so. In *Season In, Season Out*, Jack Gaver commented that almost every line in *The Toilet* had an obscenity, and that if these had been cut, it "would have left a script about two pages long." Gaver also said that people were asking how the vulgarity, obscenity, and blasphemy in the theater could be stopped, but that he felt that censorship would not be the answer. Although the constant repetition of the words in *The Toilet* made them lose their shock value, the muddled filth and profanity angered many theatergoers. In defending his scatalogical dialogue, Jones said, "The lies of today begin with the lies of language." After seeing the Jones plays, Norman Nadel, drama critic of the *New York World Telegram and Sun,* wrote two columns about obscenity. One column was titled "A Matter of Taste, Not Obscenity"; in the second column, Nadel asked, "How much will we tolerate?"

The Toilet ran into censorship problems in cities where local officials had more authority than the New York commissioner. In Boston, for example, the censor could function very much like the Lord Chamberlain in London by demanding cuts. Joseph DiCarlo, the New York Commissioner of Licenses at the time the Jones plays were produced, said that although he had the power to revoke licenses, he could never do so on the charge of objectionable dialogue. DiCarlo said he had received complaints about the plays, but that he had no legal authority to censor. Moreover, if he tried to close a play, the case would be appealed, and if he demanded cuts, he was certain the publicity would increase box office sales.

The police vice squad in Los Angeles brought charges of obscenity against *The Toilet,* but even though the case did not stand up in court, the police still held up the production on grounds of improper licensing of the theater until the police commissioner finally permitted *The Toilet* to open. One theater in Los Angeles, nevertheless, canceled its booking, and two newspapers refused to accept advertisements for the play. The Authors League promptly protested, claiming that the only reason for refusing to accept advertising would be obscenity in the advertisements.

Several plays produced in the 1965–1966 season incited the New York critics to denounce the increased use of obscenity in both dialogue and gestures. *Malcolm* by Edward Albee, which opened in January, 1966, was adapted from James Purdy's novel about a fifteen-year-old boy whose innocence is corrupted when he goes out into the world. At the opening performance, an actress who refused to speak one of the four-letter words in the dialogue substituted another word. Although the critics said that *Malcolm* did not resort to excessive vulgarity compared with other productions that same season, they wrote unfavorable reviews. Public response to *Malcolm* was equally unfavorable, for the play ran only seven performances. *Entertaining Mr. Sloane* by Joe Orton, which opened in October, 1965, had won the London critics' *Variety* award as the best new British play of 1964. The story of a sex-starved girl, her homosexual brother, and a murderer whom they trap and force into having sexual relationships with them, may have had cuts in London, but the New York production, which critics called salacious, was filled with vulgarities and obscenities that critics found more objectionable than those used in *Malcolm*. *Entertaining Mr. Sloane* also failed to interest New York audiences and closed after thirteen performances.

Two dramas previously presented in London and produced in New York during the 1965–1966 season further illustrated the growing permissiveness in the New York theater. *Inadmissible Evidence* by John Osborne dealt with a British attorney whose arrogance and selfishness have alienated his wife, his mistress, his daughter, and his staff. He has no friends, and he sees nothing ahead but spiritual destruction. Before he agreed to license the play for public performances in London, the Lord Chamberlain ordered a great many cuts in passages that he thought were offensive, particularly those that resorted to earthy vulgarities or made direct references to sexual practices, including a reference to forced sexual intercourse during menstrual periods as grounds for divorce, even though the statement was phrased in legal language that the average theater patron did not understand. In the New York production, which opened in November, 1965, and closely followed the printed text of the play, apparently most of the deleted passages had been restored. *The Persecution and Assassination of Marat as Performed by the Inmates of Charenton under the Direction of the Marquis de Sade* by Peter Weiss, in an English version by Geoffrey Skelton with verse adaptation by Adrian Mitchell, was produced in New York in December, 1965, by the David Merrick Arts Foundation, by arrangement with the Royal Shakespeare Theater of Stratford-on-Avon. In the play, usually referred to simply as *Marat/Sade,* Marat was confined to a bathtub because of a skin disease, but in one scene in the New York production, Marat appeared to be nude on stage as he crept back into the tub. Ian Richardson, who played Marat, explained in an interview that he was not completely nude, for he wore the equivalent of a burlesque stripteaser's G-string, but it was invisible to the audience. In the London production, however, Marat was fully clothed.

When the *Folies Bergère* opened in New York in 1964, complete female nudity was still not permitted on stage. In Europe, the showgirls' costumes had been topless, but in New York the city officials ordered the girls to wear at least minimal "pasties." Censorship of nudity on the New York stage was tested again in 1966 when *Les Ballets Africains,* performed by a Guinean dance company that included female topless dancers, was scheduled to open on Broadway. In London, when *Les Ballets Africains* had been presented with women dancers nude to the waist, protests were made to the Lord Chamberlain because the dancers violated the law that specified that nudes must remain motionless on stage. An aide, whom the Lord Chamberlain sent to check on the ballet, reported that the choreography was not objectionable. No action, therefore, was taken to censor the production. In New York, after an assistant license commissioner attended a rehearsal, his department ordered the women in the company to wear brassieres. The ruling was ridiculed by columnists and comedians until Mayor John V. Lindsay announced at a press conference that the bras would not have to be worn. When *Les Ballets Africains* played a return engagement in 1968, no attempt was made to censor the costumes.

Legal action was threatened, however, when an all-girl band, which had performed topless in San Francisco, was scheduled to open in New York. At the same time, the New York repertory of the Dance Studio Group, another San Francisco Company, included a number in which both male and female dancers appeared in the nude. By the time the New York authorities arranged for warrants, both groups had left New York. The delay may have been accidental, but the warrants may also have been intended as a precautionary measure to prevent the band or dance company from playing a return engagement.

Club theaters, operating on a "for members only" policy, developed off Broadway in the 1960s. Unlike the English club theaters which were organized to present dramas banned by the Lord Chamberlain, the off Broadway clubs were formed to cut operating costs. Salaries were below the scale specified by Actors Equity and the theater unions, and productions were often experimental. One of the best known of the clubs, the La Mama Club operated by Ellen Stewart, had membership dues of one dollar, but anyone who paid the fee to see a production automatically became a member. When La Mama first presented a group of one-act plays by Jean-Claude van Itallie, which later became known as *America Hurrah*, Actors Equity notified Ellen Stewart that she was to pay the minimum wage scale because she charged admissions. Since the one dollar fee collected as dues did not even cover production costs, the production was closed.

America Hurrah, a triple bill of one-act plays by van Itallie, was then produced in November, 1966, at the Pocket Theater. All three plays dealt with actions and attitudes in American life that cause people to lose their pride. *Motel*, the most controversial of the three plays, satirized motel owners and guests. Three grotesque, larger-than-life, papier-mâché dolls represent a motel owner, who talks incessantly about the luxuries of her establishment, and two guests— a man and a woman—who make love, scribble filth and draw obscenities on the walls, and wreck the motel while the owner keeps babbling about her establishment.

In London, *America Hurrah* opened to excellent reviews at the

Royal Court Theater with club performances limited to members, but the Lord Chamberlain banned it for public performances because he objected to the obscenity in *Motel*. Since another drama was scheduled to open at the Royal Court, the manager wanted to transfer *America Hurrah* to the Vaudeville Theater, but, to avoid a conflict with the censor, he tried to make it a private club theater. The Lord Chamberlain wrote to Jack Gatti, owner of the Vaudeville, and explained that he would be violating the law because it required more time to organize a club membership legally than had been allowed. When Gatti was told that he might lose his theater license, he decided not to permit *America Hurrah* to open at his theater.

In New York, on the other hand, no attempt was made to censor the triple bill. Moreover, at the end of the season, *America Hurrah* received twelve points in the first voting for the Critics Circle Award for best play of the year. Jean-Claude van Itallie, as author of *America Hurrah,* received a Drama Desk–Vernon Rice award, given for off Broadway achievement; *America Hurrah* won an Outer Circle Award, given by critics who review New York productions for out-of-town publications; and the La Mama troupe received a special Obie Award, given for off Broadway excellence, for the repertory program that it had presented to European audiences.

Complete male nudity was still taboo on the New York stage when *You Know I Can't Hear You When the Water's Running,* a program of four one-act plays by Robert Anderson, opened in March, 1967. One of the plays, *The Shock of Recognition,* dealt with a playwright who wants an actor to appear completely naked on stage facing the audience, and the playwright becomes embarrassed when he interviews an actor, obviously wrong for the role, who begins taking off his clothes. In 1967, the situation seemed highly improbable, but within three years, it was no longer shocking or even exaggerated, for complete nudity had become acceptable in the theater.

By the 1967–1968 season, there was no longer any official censorship in Boston. Audiences, however, still acted as unofficial censors for at least two productions that they felt went beyond the limits of decency. *The Balcony* by Jean Genet, translated by Bernard Frechtman, had been produced in New York at the Circle in the Square Theater in 1960. The play was set in a brothel where men assumed the roles of people they had always wanted to be, such as generals, judges, archbishops, etc. After the real Chief of Police and the men in the brothel put down a revolution taking place in the outside world, the men become the public officials they had formerly pretended to be. When the play was produced in Boston at the Charles Playhouse in 1966, a great many people walked out on *The Balcony* in protest.

Bostonians were even more vehement in their condemnation of *Little Murders,* an offbeat, bizarre farce by Jules Feiffer, which tried out in Boston. The plot involved a father who is upset because his son is a homosexual and his daughter has married a pacifist who refuses to fight hoodlums even when he is attacked. Bullets start flying in the windows, the daughter is killed, and the rest of the family, including the son-in-law, fight back. During the tryout, Bostonians who objected to the dialogue as well as to the plot not only walked out on the performance but also notified the Theatre Guild, which had produced *Little Murders,* to cancel their subscription memberships. *Little Murders* opened in New York in April, 1967, and received derogatory reviews. Feiffer denounced the critics, but audiences agreed with the negative reviews and the play closed after seven performances. That same summer, however, the Royal Shakespeare Company's production of *Little Murders* in London was successful, and, two years later, when the drama was revived off Broadway, it played to receptive audiences for four hundred performances.

The Negro Ensemble Company, operating under a grant of approximately $500,000 from the Ford Foundation, was recognized in 1967 as the first major all-Negro company organized by Negroes. The group had been in existence for several years, but in 1967, Douglas Turner Ward, the artistic director, and Robert Hooks, the executive director, had established the company as a Negro-oriented repertory and training group. During the 1967–1968 season the repertory included three plays. The first, *Song of the Lusitanian Bogey* by Peter Weiss, translated from the German by Lee Baxandall, was set in Africa and exposed Portugal's brutality in dealing with its colonies. For the second play, a revival of *Summer of the 17th Doll* by Ray Lawler, the locale was shifted from Australia to Louisiana. *Kongi's Harvest* by Wole Soyinka, a Nigerian, contrasted the customs of modern Africa with those of an earlier period.

The Negro Ensemble Company, however, met with strong opposition, particularly from black activists who condemned Douglas Turner Ward and Robert Hooks, the directors, for trying to perform like a white company. Le Roi Jones, the black playwright, who argued that blacks should avoid any connection with the white theater world, also derided Ward and Hooks, not because they had accepted money from a white foundation but because they had said they would hire white actors if the need ever arose. In retaliation, several critics pointed out that an all-Negro company was just as discriminatory as an all-white company. Ward and Hooks said their first concern was to find employment for Negroes, but they also pointed out that their first play, *Song of the Lusitanian Bogey,* was written by a white man. In spite of the controversy, at the end of the 1967–1968 season the Negro Ensemble Company received a Drama Desk–Vernon Rice Award for its contribution to the off Broadway theater, and Moses Gunn, a member of the group, received an Obie Award as a distinguished off Broadway performer.

Ceremonies in Dark Old Men by Lonne Elder III, produced in February, 1969, concerned a former dancer, now an unsuccessful barber in Harlem, who cannot prevent his children from becoming involved in crime and vice. Even objectors to the Negro Ensemble

Company's policy of using a permanent black company to produce black-oriented plays agreed that *Ceremonies in Dark Old Men* was a compassionate, well-produced drama. Lonne Elder III won both the Drama Desk and Outer Circle Awards, and *Ceremonies in Dark Old Men,* with fourteen points, was the third-ranking play in the competition for the Critics Circle Award. At the end of the 1968–1969 season, the Negro Ensemble Company received a special Tony Award for its achievements.

Although censorship in New York was becoming a rarity, it was still functioning in the other Eastern cities. After the Philadelphia newspapers printed the story that the John B. Kelly Playhouse in the Park had canceled two shows, *The Three Penny Opera* and *Sunday in New York,* Mayor H. J. Tate denied charges that he had set himself up as a censor for the playhouse and had banned the two productions. *The Three Penny Opera* was running at the Music Circus in Lambertsville, New Jersey, at the time the two productions were canceled, and the New Jersey management immediately began advertising *The Three Penny Opera* as "banned in Philadelphia." Motion picture houses in Philadelphia booked the film version of the opera, and the Society Hill Playhouse added the musical to its schedule. A news story quoted Mrs. Thrasher, managing director of the Park Playhouse, as having said that Mayor Tate had been responsible for the cancellations, but Mrs. Thrasher denied making such a statement and said that she had received no orders from Mayor Tate. Once again the Mayor denied that he had banned the productions, but the plays were not presented that summer. The Civil Liberties Union of Greater Philadelphia tried to investigate the censorship but could get no further information, and the Philadelphia newspapers summarized the situation with such comments as "Who threw that knife?"

All through the 1960s, American labor unions protested against importing English plays with scenery, costumes, and lighting intact because they could be produced at one-third the cost in England.

In retaliation against restrictions on American actors being employed abroad, the unions asked for tighter regulations on foreign actors employed in the United States. By the end of the 1963–1964 season, Actors Equity, demanding new four-year contracts, staged a one-day strike, canceling matinees of two shows. Equity also stipulated that a ratio of seventy per cent American actors to thirty per cent alien actors be reestablished because other countries had refused to permit a higher ratio of American performers. In February, 1967, forty-eight American actors picketed Lincoln Center in protest against the English actors who were appearing in plays at the Vivian Beaumont Theater. Equity members voted 491 to 2 to require producers to get permission from Equity before hiring foreign actors for Broadway or Lincoln Center productions. This ruling, however, did not apply to Canadian actors.

Actors Equity again staged protests against British actors appearing in American productions in the 1967–1968 season, and an actors' strike, which started June 18, 1967, and closed nineteen shows, was settled overnight at Gracie Mansion with Mayor Lindsay supervising the negotiations. Minimum wages were raised; alien actors could not be hired to replace American actors; and all disputes about foreign actors were to be settled by arbitration.

On November 7, 1967, Actors Equity tried to stop *The Promise* by Aleksei Arbuzov, translated by Ariadne Nicolaeff, when it opened in New York featuring three English actors, Eileen Atkins, Ian McShane, and Ian McKellen. There were no objections to the play itself, which concerned a love triangle that developed when two boys and a girl meet in Leningrad during a bombing siege. The girl marries one man, who leaves her when he realizes that she has fallen in love with the other man. The play had been a success in London, but on the opening night in New York it drew little attention inside the theater. Outside the theater, however, it made headlines, for Actors Equity staged its protest against the all-English cast by setting up a picket line, and the demonstration developed into a free-for-all that injured several bystanders. *The Promise* failed to interest audiences and could have closed within a week, but the producers forced a run of twenty-three performances to insure the sale of motion picture rights.

Arguments between producers and Actors Equity over hiring foreign actors reached an impasse in October, 1968, over the comedy *Rockefeller and the Red Indians* by Ray Galton and Alan Simpson, which had been produced in London as *The Wind in the Sassafras Tree*. Equity protested against the all-English cast but producer David Merrick insisted that comedian Frankie Howerd and the other English actors were essential to the play. Although Norman Nadel, who was called in as arbitrator, sided with Equity, a compromise was finally reached with Merrick being permitted to star Howerd in the comedy which satirized western movies and television programs. The controversy did little to stir up public interest, for *Rockefeller and the Red Indians* ran only four performances.

In 1968, the New York theater began breaking precedents in presenting obscenity, nudity, and simulated sex acts on stage. Many producers believed that Mayor John V. Lindsay did not want to interfere with the theater, for city police and the Commissioner of Licenses did not follow through on protests made by groups denouncing the increased permissiveness in the theater. This apparent hands-off policy by city officials was evident in several off Broadway productions. *Tom Paine* by Paul Foster, a drama about the American Revolutionary figure, produced by the La Mama troupe in March, 1968, included one scene in which both men and women in the cast wore transparent gauzy cloaks but otherwise were completely nude. Most of the reviews, with the exception of the one printed in the *Village Voice,* the Greenwich Village newspaper, made little or no comment on the nudity. The La Mama troupe had previously presented the play none too successfully in London and in Edinburgh. In London, the play closed after thirty-four performances; in New York, it ran 295.

Scuba Duba by Bruce Jay Friedman, produced in October, 1967, presented the frustrations of a white man trying to cope with a faithless wife whose lover is a black intellectual. As a token of the new freedom in the theater, *Scuba Duba* included a scene in which a frowsy blonde, nude to the waist, wandered on stage supposedly looking for a glass of warm milk.

Off Broadway productions with references to homosexuality and lesbianism were not only more common but were now also winning major drama awards. *Your Own Thing,* based on Shakespeare's *Twelfth Night,* with book by Donald Driver and music and lyrics by Danny Apolinar and Hal Lester, won the Critics Circle Award as the best musical of the year. Driver's updated version still dealt with a twin brother and sister, Sebastian and Viola, who are shipwrecked in Illyria, neither knowing the other is alive, but Driver gave the comedy a new twist by having Viola and Sebastian wear a unisex costume so that they not only dressed alike but also looked alike. The other characters, therefore, do not know that Viola is a girl. Orson falls in love with Viola but feels guilty about his affection because he thinks she is a boy. Instead of objecting to the homosexual implication, most of the critics credited Driver with making the boy-likes-boy story amusing rather than offensive and called *Your Own Thing* the best modern variation of a Shakespearean play that had been produced in years.

In March, 1968, the American Place Theater presented a bill of three one-act plays by Ed Bullins with all-Negro casts. The original title, *The Electronic Nigger and Others,* was later changed to *Three Plays* by Ed Bullins. At the end of the season, the triple bill received a Drama Desk–Vernon Rice Award for "outstanding contribution to the off Broadway theater." One of the three plays, *Clara's Ole Man,* dealt with a young man who calls on an attractive girl and then discovers that her "ole man" is a domineering lesbian.

The Beard by Michael McClure involved two characters who represent Jean Harlow and Billy the Kid. They meet in eternity and discuss sex in four-letter obscenities and vulgarities, and the play ends in a symbolic act of sexual perversion. When *The Beard* first opened in 1966 in San Francisco, the police, who had filmed and taped a performance, arrested the two actors on charges of obscenity. The actors were later acquitted and the play reopened in 1967 without further interference. *The Beard* then opened off Broadway in October, 1967, to very poor reviews. The *New Yorker* magazine, deeming the play unworthy of review, ignored it completely; the *New York Times* refused to print an advertisement, which it considered improper because it included a quote with sexual references. New Yorkers would not have been surprised if the play had closed and the actors had been arrested, but the police did not stop the production, which folded after an unsatisfactory run of one hundred performances. At the end of the season, Rip Torn, as director of *The Beard,* won an Obie award for off Broadway achievement. When *The Beard* opened in Los Angeles in 1968, the actors, director, and producer were arrested on twelve charges of obscenity. A local judge ruled that the Los Angeles ordinance requiring a police permit to present a stage play or motion picture constituted a restraint of free speech. The obscenity charges, nevertheless, were not dropped, and the show remained closed.

Several Broadway productions, which also broke former barriers, were less controversial than the off Broadway shows. *The Seven Descents of Myrtle* by Tennessee Williams, produced in 1968, included a reference to a perverted sex act. The *Prime of Miss Jean Brodie* by Jay Allen, which had first been presented in London, was somewhat revised for the American production in 1968. The scene showing a young schoolgirl posing topless for her married lover, an artist, however, was the same in both productions.

New York officials did not take action against any of these productions, either on or off Broadway, nor did the commissioner of licenses threaten to padlock any theaters. Ephraim London, a New York attorney who had handled a number of cases dealing with obscenity, was quoted in a news item in *Variety* as having said that several plays produced in 1968 would probably have been banned five years earlier, and that *The Beard* would probably have been padlocked as late as 1966. Ephraim London also said that it had become difficult to get convictions on charges of obscenity because decisions handed down by local, federal, and even the United States Supreme Court, legally defined obscenity in general rather than in specific terms. The word *obscenity,* therefore, was often too broad to be applied to plays that might be considered obscene for a number of different reasons. Joel Tyler, the New York Commissioner of Licenses, said that he could not revoke a license until the police had made an arrest and obtained a conviction. The legal terminology of the court decision, however, hampered the New York police who said that even if the public strongly protested against a play, they would hesitate to take action, for they could not be sure that any charges they made against the play would be valid. Adding to the confusion were several critics who opposed censorship of any kind and championed such productions as *Hair* for breaking down barriers and giving the theater more freedom.

Hair, subtitled "The American Tribal Love Rock Musical," with book and lyrics by Gerome Ragni and James Rado and music by Galt MacDermot, opened off Broadway on October 29, 1967, at Joseph Papp's New York Shakespeare Festival Public Theater and closed on December 10, 1967, after forty-nine performances. The production, directed by Gerald Freedman, included a teen-age love story, the revolt of modern youth, the generation gap between parents and children, and the plight of a young hippie who is drafted and cannot decide whether to burn his draft card. He goes into the army, is sent to Vietnam, and is killed. On December 22, 1967, *Hair* reopened at the Cheetah, a nightclub, and ran forty-five performances, closing January 28, 1968. Since the Cheetah required arena-type staging, *Hair* was less effective than it had been at Papp's Public Theater. It still, however, had emotional appeal in depicting the revolt of the young hippies against the conventional standards of their parents and against the Vietnam war.

After *Hair* closed at the Cheetah, producer Michael Butler took over the musical and decided to bring it to Broadway in a revised version. He signed Tom O'Horgan to direct the new *Hair* in which the plot was virtually eliminated. New songs were added along with multiple references to sex, politics, drugs, pollution, and religion. Also added were overtones of homosexuality and a controversial new scene at the end of the first act in which both men and women appeared totally nude facing the audience. In *The Season,* William Goldman said that when he saw *Hair* at a preview performance on Broadway, the stage lights were not dimmed, but at the official Broadway opening performance on April 29, 1968, the lights were definitely dimmed. According to press reports, the entire cast did not appear in the nude. Only those actors or actresses who felt like doing so at any performance shed their costumes. During the preview performances, columnists made frequent references to the nude scene and speculated about whether the police would close the show, but *Hair* opened without any official interference.

The reviews ranged from poor to ecstatic. Some critics condemned *Hair* for its irreverence, vulgarity, and nudity, which they felt should have been cut (as it was later in several censored versions). Others called *Hair* amateurish and repetitive. Still others said the lyrics were unintelligible. Even devotees of the show admitted that it took several hearings to catch all the words, a fact that may have explained the phenomenal sale of record albums made by the original cast. On the other hand, those critics who liked *Hair* wrote in superlatives calling it a significant production that unshackled the American stage by breaking down former taboos. The majority of the television critics also hailed *Hair* as a superior musical. Their comments, in fact, were quoted most frequently in the advertisements. Critics who had seen both the original off Broadway production and the revised Broadway version commented that the story line in the original version had aroused more sympathy for the characters; the Broadway version emphasized the jeering and antagonistic attitude of rebellious hippies. The critics in general, however, agreed that the best part of *Hair* was its excellent score. At the end of the first season, in a poll of the New York drama critics taken by *Variety* magazine, Galt MacDermot received the highest number of votes (eight) as best composer for *Hair*; Gerome Ragni and James Rado received the highest number of votes (seven) as best lyricists.

Hair drew capacity audiences in New York even though the reactions of audiences were as varied as the opinions of the critics. People who liked *Hair* thought it typified the revolt of modern youth; those who hated it walked out on the show. *Hair* made theatrical headlines when multiple road companies began extended engagements that drew capacity houses. By 1970, *Hair* had become an international success with twenty-three companies touring in ten countries. The nude scene, however, was not included in some of the foreign productions.

In New York, Michael Butler had no apparent trouble with censorship although the production did break into the news when an astronaut walked out of the theater in protest during a scene in which the American flag was desecrated. Butler, however, not only fired Rado and Ragni, the authors, who played leading roles, but also barred them from coming into the theater because they were reportedly "experimenting with new material." A former member of the New York company later said Butler had taken this action because the actors had tried to make the nude scene pornographic by painting parts of their bodies. Butler, Rado, and Ragni later resolved their differences when Rado and Ragni agreed to proper procedures before introducing new material. They were then permitted to return to the cast. By December, 1971, *Hair* began operating in New York on cut rates but did not close until July, 1972, with a run of 1,750 consecutive performances.

Outside of New York, on the other hand, *Hair* met strong opposition from censors. In Mexico, the production closed after the first performance. In 1969, when the United States military forces were accused of banning *Hair,* Frank Kinsman, the field programming director for the army, said that *Hair* and similar offensive productions had been declared unfit for G.I. theaters because it was "good judgment" to avoid presenting productions that could cause trouble. He also added that if requests had been made for *Hair* to be produced at a G.I. theater, the revue more than likely would have been revised and several scenes would have been cut. *Hair* ran into censorship problems in several cities such as Indianapolis, South Bend, and Evansville; it had similar problems in St. Paul, Minnesota, and San Antonio, Texas. *Hair* also ran into difficulties in Los Angeles in 1969, for it triggered a series of raids by police who cracked down on the growing fad of nude dancers and made fifty arrests. The police action, however, did not stop *Hair* or the other shows, for although the city ordinance authorized the officers to make arrests, it did not give them the power to close productions or padlock theaters.

In Boston, *Hair* had an advance sale of $600,000 when the district attorney ordered the production to be closed. The local authorities had attended the first preview and, according to a report in *Variety,* the Boston commissioner of licenses had objected to the nudity, the obscenity, and the manner in which the American flag was desecrated. The district attorney did not enforce the closing order until seven judges of the Massachusetts Supreme Court saw a performance. They also demanded cuts including the nude scene and the flag episode. When the producer refused to cut the sex scenes and eliminate the nudity, the district attorney closed the show. The producer immediately filed an appeal with the Federal Courts but the cost involved was staggering. He not only had to refund all the money for the huge advance ticket sales but also had to defray running expenses while waiting for the court's decision. Although a panel of three federal judges ruled in favor of *Hair*, the Boston district attorney prevented the show from reopening by taking his case to the United States Supreme Court. Six weeks after the closing, the Supreme Court handed down a decision made by only eight justices instead of the customary nine. The tie vote was interpreted as a legal technicality: although the decision of the federal panel was not overridden, the tie vote indicated that the decision was not upheld either. The way was cleared, therefore, for *Hair* to reopen and continue playing in Boston to capacity houses.

The acceptance of nudity on stage gradually spread to other cities. During its road tour in the United States, the Royal Shakespeare Company presented *Dr. Faustus* with a nude but gilded Helen of Troy wearing only a tiara, but the production apparently aroused little or few complaints from city officials. In Detroit, for example, there was only minor newspaper comment on the nudity, and the city police took no action against the play.

Although *Hair* broke down barriers in presenting nudity on the Broadway stage, a number of off Broadway and off off Broadway productions during this same period were even more audacious than *Hair*. Most of these shows were presented in club theaters or playhouses, which did not operate on a regular eight-performances-weekly schedule. In *Best Plays of 1967–1968*, R. J. Schroeder cited some of the following off off Broadway productions in which the nudity was accentuated. At the Cooper Arts Theater, which operated only on weekends, *Christmas Turkey* by Ed Cooke featured an actress completely nude, in full stage lighting, who faced the audience in most of her scenes. At the Extension Theater, which presented plays from Wednesday through Sunday for two or three weeks, the heroine in *Shower* by Ron Tavel played many of her scenes almost nude in the audience section of the theater. *The Shirt* by Leonard Melfi, presented at the La Mama club theater, featured a rapist who doffed all of his clothing except a symbolic shirt before attacking one of the actresses. In *Tennis, Anyone?* by F. V. Hunt, produced at the Troupe Repertory Theater Club, which operated usually on weekends, a woman is raped and then proceeds to play the rest of the act without trying to put on the clothing the rapist had torn off. At the Bouwerie Lane Theater, the Play-House of the Ridiculous presented an extended engagement of *Conquest of the Universe* by Charles Ludlam, with music by John Vaccaro, in which five actresses performed in the nude. Schroeder also reported that the *Village Voice,* the Greenwich Village newspaper, started to run advertisements that included only the title of a show, the name and location of the theater, and a picture of the type of nudity being presented.

The breakthrough in nudity and dialogue became evident in several revivals produced in New York in the 1969–1970 season. *Fortune and Men's Eyes* by John Herbert, originally produced in 1947, had dealt with the emotional pressures and homosexual experiences of four inmates in a Canadian prison—a dyed blonde; his young, idealistic victim; a rough man who protests that he is not a homosexual; and a farm boy. When the revival opened off Broadway in 1969, several New York critics objected to it not only because it included nudity but also because it emphasized homosexuality in several explicit scenes. *Dark of the Moon* by Howard Richardson and William Berney, originally produced in 1945, dealt with John, a witch boy, who enters into a compact with a conjur woman to make him human so that he can marry Barbara, a human. John agrees that if Barbara is unfaithful to him within a year, he will renounce his humanness and return to the witch tribe. Barbara's Christian relatives persuade her to break the witch's spell by having an affair with another human, Marvin Hudgens. Barbara dies and John returns to his tribe. When the revival opened in April, 1970, with several nude scenes, particularly those involving witches, that had not been in the original Broadway production, the critics, instead of objecting, said the nudity was appropriate in creating the mood of mystic witchcraft.

New plays of the 1969–1970 season included *And Puppy Dog Tails* by David Gaard, produced off Broadway, involving a homosexual love triangle played partly in the nude. *Grin and Bare It!* by Ken McGuire, adapted from a play by Tom Cushing, opened on Broadway and closed in less than two weeks. The comedy dealt with a girl who brings her fiancé home to meet the members of her family, all nudists. In his Broadway report in *Best Plays of 1969–1970*, Otis L. Guernsey, Jr., commented that it was worth mentioning that the actors who had performed completely in the nude wore dressing gowns for the curtain calls to show that they were "actors playing naked *characters*. As soon as they stepped out of character, they clothed themselves."

During this same season, John Chapman, drama critic for the *New York Daily News*, had become surfeited with plays dealing with homosexuality. He therefore did not review such plays as the revival of *Fortune and Men's Eyes; Spitting Image*, a comedy in which a homosexual couple have a baby; *Boys in the Band*, which depicted the bitterness and deceit among a group of homosexuals attending a birthday party; and *Geese*, two one-act plays dealing with homosexuality and lesbianism.

Although there were no major public protests against the increased nudity and homosexuality on stage, the off Broadway productions which had nude scenes or dealt with homosexuality began reaching a saturation point, for many of the producers were charging higher prices than the current ticket scale on Broadway. The limited number of people who were willing to pay ten dollars or more per ticket was not sufficient to keep all the plays running.

Despite the permissiveness in the New York theater, there were still occasional flare-ups and protests against dramas dealing with controversial political issues. *The Cuban Thing* by Jack Gelber, which opened and closed on the same night, September 24, 1968, dealt with the Cuban revolution and a family that learns to accept Castro and his political beliefs. Anti-Castro protestors were sufficiently incited to stage a demonstration outside the theater; critics said the demonstration was far more interesting than the play.

In New York, *The Soldiers* by Rolf Hochhuth, translated by Robert D. MacDonald, did not stir up the same storm of protests as Hochhuth's earlier drama, *The Deputy,* although the official reaction to *The Soldiers* in England indicated that it could have met with similar opposition in the United States. In *The Soldiers,* Hochhuth alleged that Sir Winston Churchill, who wanted Russia's cooperation in World War II, had supported Stalin's demands for extensive bombings of German cities in 1943. The play also accused Churchill of complicity in the supposed murder of General Sikorski, former Prime Minister and head of the exiled Polish government during World War II. Michael White, in partnership with Kenneth Tynan, had planned to produce *The Soldiers* at the National Theater in London, but the board of directors of the theater disapproved of the drama. Laurence Olivier, artistic director of the National Theater, then wanted to produce *The Soldiers* as a private venture, but the Lord Chamberlain refused to permit the play to be staged unless the heirs of Sir Winston Churchill and other people represented in the drama gave their approval. *The Soldiers,* therefore, was first produced in Toronto and then brought to New York on May 1, 1968, in a slightly revised production. There were no official protests against the drama, but the New York critics, who disapproved of the play for its untheatrical quality rather than its plot, thought the charges against Sir Winston Churchill were unconvincing and implausible. New York audiences agreed with the critics, and *The Soldiers* closed on Broadway after a short run of twenty-two performances, a financial failure.

By way of contrast, when *The Soldiers* was later produced in London, Edward Prchal, the Czech pilot whose plane had crashed in 1943 killing General Sikorski, brought suit against Hochhuth, claiming that the play suggested he had been involved with Prime Minister Churchill in the plot to murder General Sikorski. Early in 1972, the British High Court ruled that Rolf Hochhuth was to pay costs plus damages of approximately twenty-five thousand pounds to Prchal. Michael White and Kenneth Tynan, coproducers, and Clifford Williams, director of the play, were also ordered to pay Prchal a substantial sum. In summing up the libel action, Justice Bean told the jury that a man of Sir Winston Churchill's stature did not need defense against this type of attack, but that Prchal, who could be the victim of the wrong type of publicity, did need support. In spite of the court order, Prchal was unable to collect any damages from the dramatist, for Hochhuth, who lived in Switzerland, was not subject to the orders of the British High Court so long as he stayed out of England.

An off Broadway production broke another taboo by dramatizing a form of bestiality in *Futz!* by Rochelle Owens. The play, which had been part of the La Mama repertory for a year, had also been presented in Edinburgh and in London, where it was given at a private club theater. After the London opening, Frank Marcus, drama critic for the London *Sunday Telegraph* said, "There were inaudible intakes of breath from the London audiences" at the profusion of four-letter words and the simulated sex scenes. The plot dealt with Cyrus Futz, whose unnatural love for his pig, Amanda, shocks the community. At the end of the play, both Cyrus and the pig are killed. When a revised version opened in New York in 1968, most of the critics had little to say about *Futz!* other than to comment that it was poorly written or that the original off Broadway La Mama production had been better. One critic, however, named *Futz!* as his third choice for the Critics Circle Award as the best play of the year.

Nudity in off Broadway productions became so prevalent that actors protested to Equity that they be notified if they would be acting in the nude before they auditioned for roles. Not content with having actors appear in the nude, the Living Theater went one step further by having the nude actors not only talk to members of the audience but also invite them to come on stage, remove their clothing, and join the actors. Julian Beck and Judith Malina, producers and directors of the Living Theater, had been abroad with their company and had served short jail terms after their return to New York for convictions of tax evasion in the 1965–1966 season. They resumed full scale operations in 1968–1969 with a repertory that included *Frankenstein, Mysteries and Smaller Pieces, The Antigone of Sophokles* adapted by Judith Malina from Brecht's adaptation, and *Paradise Now,* the play that created the most discussion. When the Living Theater offered its program at Yale, drama critics said the plays were basically static. The Living Theater then opened an engagement at the Brooklyn Academy of Music, and New Yorkers who saw the productions agreed with Walter Kerr, Sunday drama critic for the *New York Times,* who denounced *Paradise Now.* Julian Beck, in turn, denounced Kerr and blamed the poor review on Kerr's refusal to accept the actors' invitation to come on stage and take off his clothing. Beck's illogical attack on Kerr won few, if any, supporters from the other drama critics.

Critics who did not oppose the increased nudity, obscenity, and perversion maintained that the theater was developing new freedom in art; dissenters argued that exhibitionism on stage lacked taste and was definitely not art. The limits of permissiveness on the New York stage were apparently reached when the New York police closed the off off Broadway production of *Che!* by Lennox Raphael, in which nudity, explicit sex acts, a nymphomaniac nun, the character of Che Guevara, and the president of the United States were all jumbled together. Advance publicity boasted that the play would not only include nude scenes but also that the actors playing Che and the Nun would actually perform the sex act rather than simulate it. In his *Best Plays of 1968–1969,* Otis L. Guernsey, Jr., raised the question, "Is there a borderline between art and reality," and then added, "Even Nero would have agreed that murders should be mimed, not performed." In commenting on the fact that offending people was not sufficient reason for censorship, Guernsey also asked if it would be a curtailment of art to have the sex act simulated.

After the opening performance of *Che!* at the Free Store Theater on March 24, 1969, a criminal court justice signed an arrest warrant for the cast, the producers, the crew, and other people connected with the production on such charges as consensual sodomy, public lewdness, obscenity, and impairing the morals of a minor.

The crackdown on *Che!* was the first such action taken by the police since Mayor Lindsay had taken office in 1966. The defendants were released on bail, and the play might have continued while the case was brought to trial, but to avoid further nightly arrests, *Che!* was closed temporarily. It soon reopened at much higher admission prices while the controversy continued over the right of censors to "curb artistic freedom." An editorial in the *New York Times* stated, "This explicit portrayal on the stage of sexual intercourse is the final step in the erosion of taste and subtlety in the theater." Most of the critics said the play, in spite of its attempted sensationalism, was boring and dull. Martin Gottfried, critic for *Women's Wear Daily,* who called the show "tacky and pretty innocent," was more appalled by the actions of the audience, including amateur photographers who were trying to get close-up action shots, than he was by the antics of the cast. Other writers said that *Che!* might have died a quick death if it had not been given so much publicity, for it was merely a flimsy political satire. New York Police Inspector Joseph Fink also said he thought it had been wrong to close the play because the police still had no guidelines or definitions of just what constituted obscenity or pornography on the stage.

While charges against those who were arrested were still pending, a hearing was held in the United States District Court. The Manhattan district attorney and representatives from the police department were asked to justify why they should be permitted to stop performances of the play. The situation was publicized in the newspapers and broadcasting media, and reporters indicated that the federal judge would probably decide against *Che!*. The critics, in summarizing the possible outcome of the case, commented that if the actors in *Che!* were required to be fully clothed, the play would be even duller than it was. The Manhattan Criminal Court later ruled that *Che!*, which included twenty-three sex acts, was obscene without redeeming value. The author, producer, and other personnel were fined, although the decision was appealed. The ruling against *Che!* encouraged those who advocated censorship to continue their battle to curb the trend toward pornography in the theater. Several producers became more cautious, but the nudity and obscenity, in general, did not stop. *Che!* reopened later with the sex acts supposedly toned down and with the actors wearing some semblance of a costume, but the play soon dropped into oblivion. On the other hand, the Free Store Theater, which had gained notoriety by presenting *Che!*, was now operating with the highest off off Broadway price scale and was presenting shows for as many performances, often with more than one given on the same night, as was profitable.

While the litigation involving *Che!* was in progress, Hillard Elkins was preparing to produce *Oh! Calcutta!*, a revue of erotica, in which the cast would appear, for the most part, completely nude on a fully lighted stage. Elkins, who objected to newspaper stories that linked *Oh! Calcutta!* with *Che!*, said his production differed from Lennox Raphael's play and did not include the sex act.

The police action against *Che!*, however, alerted Elkins, for he asked city officials to attend a preview performance, presumably to determine whether *Oh! Calcutta!* would run into problems with the commissioner of licenses or with the police. The move was strategic, for *Oh! Calcutta!* was permitted to open off Broadway at the Eden Theater without any interference from authorities even though the revue, in spite of Elkins's preproduction statement, did include several sketches in which the nude actors satirized the sex act. Tickets at the Eden, which had a seating capacity of 499, were priced at twenty-five dollars for the first two rows; most of the remaining seats were fifteen dollars. The production, devised by Kenneth Tynan, had an impressive list of contributors, but none of them were identi-

fied with any specific sketch or routine in the program. When *Oh!
Calcutta!* opened, *Time* quoted the comment by Clive Barnes that
the revue "left nothing to the imagination." A few critics thought
Oh! Calcutta! took another step forward in liberating the theater
and that the choreography was excellent but that some of the
sketches were offensive. Most of the critics, however, condemned
the revue, not as a shocker but as a bore. Despite the negative
reviews, word-of-mouth advertising plus an excellent publicity campaign kept *Oh! Calcutta!* running two seasons before it was moved
to Broadway for another profitable extended run at lower prices.

Outside of New York, *Oh! Calcutta!* ran into censorship problems, particularly in Ottawa and in Massachusetts. Moreover, the
presentation of *Oh! Calcutta!* in motion picture theaters on closed
circuit television was a fiasco. Not only was the overpriced attraction
poorly attended, but in several cities the television tube did not work
and the admissions had to be refunded. Difficulties in booking the
picture outside of New York indicated the problems the producer
faced in booking the stage version on the road; the picture was
banned outright in some cities, and the bookings in a number of
other cities were canceled before the film was scheduled to open.

Oh! Calcutta! opened in London after censorship had been
abolished in 1968. The preview performances were sell-outs with
ticket brokers asking and getting under-the-counter premiums as
high as eighteen and twenty pounds per ticket. The demand for
seats may have been prompted by a rumor that the revue, in spite
of the Act of 1968, could run into censorship trouble for violating
the law governing pornography, but when the revue opened without
any official interference, the demand for tickets did not drop.

Another off Broadway production, *The Dirtiest Show in Town*
by Tom Eyen, which followed *Oh! Calcutta!*, also included a series
of sketches showing nude actors simulating sex, including a group
orgy. One New York critic said the show was mainly for voyeurs;
others called it a satire on sex deviations; but most of them agreed

that *The Dirtiest Show in Town* demonstrated not only how completely the theater had broken every former taboo in dialogue and action but also how little power city officials had left to censor or padlock productions.

During this same period, nevertheless, politicians and government officials were still being accused of censoring productions. Charges of censorship were made in 1969 against the Board of Directors of the Ford's Theater Society in Washington, D.C., because it had rejected *The President Is Dead* by Paul Shyre, a play dealing with the assassination of Abraham Lincoln. Shyre said that his play had shown the similarity between the assassination of President Lincoln and the murder of President Kennedy as well as the similarity to assassinations of other prominent people. According to Shyre, the play was to have opened in November at the restored Ford's Theater where Lincoln had been shot 104 years ago, but early in August, Shyre received a letter from the managing director of the theater stating that the Board felt the drama "would be inappropriate for Ford's Theater." Shyre added that his play had been rejected because he had made Secretary of War Edwin M. Stanton appear to be "too much of a villain."

The managing director of the theater said he had used the word *inappropriate* in the letter because he had tried to be diplomatic about the rejection, but that the Board's refusal to produce the play was not an act of censorship. Mrs. F. C. Hewitt, president of Ford's Theater Society, also denied the censorship charges and said that the script had been considered along with a great many other plays including classics and contemporary dramas. She further explained that when the Board of Directors discussed Shyre's drama, and questioned the historical accuracy of Shyre's characterization of Stanton and his involvement in the assassination, Theodore Mann, director of Ford's Theater, decided that the theater should not produce the play. Since the theater had not made a direct commitment to produce *The President Is Dead,* the directors felt they were within their rights in rejecting the manuscript, along with other plays that had been under consideration. People not associated with Ford's Theater agreed with the directors that refusal of a script did not constitute censorship, and that historical inaccuracy was a justifiable reason for rejection.

On March 8, 1972, however, the Ford's Theater Society, in association with Frank Connelly and Gerald Roberts presented the world premiere of another play by Paul Shyre, *An Unpleasant Evening with H. L. Mencken,* which Shyre had adapted from writings by Mencken. The production featuring David Wayne ran twenty-three performances.

A more complicated problem developed when the United States Department of State considered sponsoring a Middle and Far Eastern tour of avant-garde short plays, which had been produced in Los Angeles under the supervision of Gordon Davidson in the Mark Taper Forum's "New Theater for Now" series. The program for the 1969–1970 series included plays by James Bridges, Jules Feiffer, Israel Horovitz, Adrienne Kennedy, Jack Larson, Terrence McNally, Leonard Melfi, Robert Patrick, Harvey Perr, Sharon Thie, Jean-Claude van Itallie, and Lanford Wilson. Several plays were selected and placed in rehearsal, but less than two weeks before the tour was to begin, the State Department canceled the project because of "unstable and changing political conditions in the host countries." The dramatists involved immediately accused the State Department of censorship, but people familiar with the situation thought it was probably not censorship that caused the cancellation so much as apprehension that the congressmen who appropriated funds for cultural programs would not approve of the dramas selected. Others familiar with the workings of Congress said the situation was similar in some respects to the cancellations made by the government in the WPA Theater project when officials maintained that the government should not finance productions that could lead to political involvements with foreign countries.

A decision handed down by the United States Supreme Court during the 1969–1970 theatrical season negated a federal statute that made it a crime for an actor to wear a United States military costume if his characterization discredited the service. The law had been invoked against a protestor, dressed in a military uniform, who had thus assumed the role of actor and put on an antiwar guerilla demonstration outside the draft induction center in Houston, Texas. Justice Hugo L. Black, in commenting on the Supreme Court's unanimous decision in favor of the "actor," said that such incidents as the demonstration might be "crude, amateurish, and perhaps unappealing," but that "an actor, like everyone else in our country, enjoys a Constitutional right to freedom of speech, including the right openly to criticize the government during a dramatic performance." Advocates for freedom in the arts hailed the decision as a decided victory, for if the decision had upheld the federal statute, it would have validated at least one type of censorship in the American theater.

11

The 1970s

IN THE 1969–1970 season, a number of poorly written attractions and "peep shows" opened both on and off Broadway with very high admission prices. Many of these attempts at eroticism, unable to compete for the limited audiences of voyeurs interested only in the nude and the crude, failed.

Advocates of censorship in the theater renewed their efforts in the 1970s to pass legislation that would curb the trend toward pornography. A bill was proposed in the New York State Legislature to ban exposure of the female body, but this was to be an amendment to the penal law already in existence and would apply not only to nudity but also to costumes that had "illegal exposure." In reporting on the proposed bill, *Variety* noted that the law presumably dealt with exposure of the female but not the male body.

During this same period, the California Supreme Court ruled by a four to three decision that stage performances were not subject to the new state laws against obscenity. According to the California Supreme Court, sections of the law were not violated by such controversial productions as *The Beard,* which had been raided by the

Los Angeles police on charges that the characters in *The Beard* behaved like sex deviates and therefore could be arrested for acting like deviates in public. By ruling that the law did not apply to the drama, the Court stripped the California police not only of the power to challenge the content of plays but also of the authority to padlock theaters for presenting objectionable plays.

Several New York critics who deplored the increased use of scatalogical dialogue said that plays could be just as vigorous if the lines were less earthy. To prove their point, they cited several earlier productions, including Neil Simon's *The Odd Couple,* which involved a group of men who did not resort to blasphemy or obscenity. Moreover, according to these critics, if the characters had used scatalogical dialogue, the play would have lost much of its humor. These critics also cited *Guys and Dolls,* in which the characters were gamblers, crap shooters, nightclub dancers, and prostitutes who not only avoided vulgarities but actually heightened the humor by speaking in euphemisms and stilted dialogue to disguise their raffishness and to give themselves an air of respectability.

In the early 1970s, the uninhibited freedom of expression was evident in the permissiveness of New York officials and in the acceptance by audiences and critics of former taboos in several productions that opened to excellent reviews and received recognition as distinguished dramas by winning major drama awards. *That Championship Season* by Jason Miller opened off Broadway on May 2, 1972, at Joseph Papp's New York Shakespeare Festival Public Theater, and at the end of the 1971–1972 season it received the New York Drama Critics Circle Award as the best play of the year. After running 144 performances, the production was moved on September 14 to the Booth Theater in the Broadway sector where it ran 700 additional performances and won both the Tony Award and the Pulitzer Prize for drama as the best play of the 1972–1973 season.

The drama dealt with four members of a 1952 basketball championship team who have an annual reunion at the home of their former coach, now retired. The four members include the town mayor who knows he will be defeated at the next election; an industrialist who realizes that people cater to him only for his money; a school official who has no hope for advancement in his position; and a man who has become an alcoholic. The coach tells the men, who are now in their thirties, that they have won more in life than the championship, but the men know he is wrong, for they realize they have lost more than they have gained. Their disillusionment is reflected in the attitude of the fifth member of the team who does not appear in the play. He has not attended the reunions because he feels the team won the championship ruthlessly, did not deserve the trophy, and should have returned it.

The dialogue in *That Championship Season,* which was a powerful drama, was far more outspoken than the dialogue in the plays of the 1920s and 1930s that the Pulitzer Committee had bypassed because they included a few salty expressions. Many of the critics made no comment about the earthiness and obscenities in the dialogue, and those critics who made casual references to it said the dialogue was vigorous, realistic, and appropriate for the characters in the play.

Grease, a musical by Jim Jacobs and Warren Casey, also opened off Broadway at the Eden Theater on February 17, 1972. It was classified as a Broadway production, however, because it was operating on Broadway contracts. On June 6, 1972, the musical moved to the Broadhurst Theater to continue its successful run. The characters in *Grease,* which satirized the Elvis Presley–James Dean–rock and roll era of the 1950s, were mainly high-school students who slicked down their hair with grease and imitated their movie star and singing idols in their walk, their talk, and their songs. An earlier musical, *Bye, Bye, Birdie,* produced in 1960, had also satirized the teenage hysteria over Elvis Presley, and mature theatergoers had laughed at the antics and harmless prattle of the adolescents. *Bye, Bye, Birdie,* however, was a fairy tale in comparison with

Grease, which amused the young people who had grown up in the late 1950s but shocked some of their parents with the references to sex and pregnancy. A number of women objected to *Grease* because the earthiness and vulgarities were spoken by girls as well as by boys. In the 1920s, the vice brigade would undoubtedly have protested against *Grease;* newspaper editorials would probably have condemned the musical and called it an insult to the youth of America. In 1972, however, the earthy language had lost its shock value for most theatergoers. The critics, for the most part, ignored the dialogue and praised *Grease* for its lampoon of the 1950s, its rhythmic score, and its exuberant young cast, particularly Barry Bostwick for his impersonation of James Dean, Adrienne Barbeau, Timothy Myers, and Carol Demas. *Grease,* which was billed as the *No, No, Nanette* of the thirty-year-olds, developed into a major musical success and, by January 1, 1977, had run over two thousand performances and was still drawing large audiences.

The Changing Room by David Storey, produced in 1972, won the New York Drama Critics Circle Award as the best play of the 1972–1973 season. The drama presented a realistic portrait of the action in a locker room before, during, and after a professional rugby game. The action emphasizes the brutality of the game and the pain the players endure from the strenuous physical beating they take on the field. As the play opens, the men come into the locker room, take off their street clothes and put on clean uniforms. During the halves, they collapse in the locker room, and after the game, they doff their uniforms, put on their street clothes, and leave. Although the men stripped to the nude as they changed in and out of their uniforms, they did so without any gestures of false modesty or any attempt to make the scene erotic. In discussing the play, Otis Guernsey, Jr., said, "This rare example of total mass male nudity on a Broadway stage was so far from being shocking, so fluent a part of the stage action, that most members of the audience didn't become conscious of it until after it was well under way." Very few of the critics or columnists made more than a casual reference to the nudity nor were there any official protests against the play, which undoubtedly would have been banned in New York as late as the early 1960s.

In the early 1970s, laws governing obscenity in books, in films, and on the stage varied from state to state, but on June 21, 1973, the United States Supreme Court handed down two rulings that established new national guidelines for the limits of sexual candor in films and books. Theatrical producers were well aware of the fact that these decisions could also apply to nudity and obscenity in stage plays. Formerly, the law governing motion pictures had specified that a film had to be declared "utterly without social redeeming value" before it could be banned, but the United States Supreme Court, after hearing several cases dealing with obscenity, handed down two major decisions. First, the word *utterly* was no longer necessary. A film, therefore, could be banned if it had "no redeeming value." Second, the Court ruled that local community standards rather than national standards should determine what constitutes pornography, thus giving each local community the power to set its own standard of censorship.

The United States Supreme Court, however, also made the following specifications: Each community must decide (1) whether the average person would find that the work appealed to prurient interests; (2) whether the sexual conduct in the work is depicted or described offensively by exceeding limits defined by individual states; and (3) whether the work lacks "serious literary, artistic, political or scientific value."

In commenting on the decisions, attorneys generally agreed that the words *serious* and *value* gave censors wider scope than the original restriction "utterly without social redeeming value."

These decisions had been based on a case in California (*Miller* v. *California*), involving a man who was prosecuted under state law for mailing obscene brochures, and on a case in Georgia that involved the showing of two films at an "adult theater." In the latter case, lawyers for the defense argued that "adult" films had constitutional rights if they were shown only to "consenting adults," but the Supreme Court ruled that each state has a right to stem "the tide of commercialized obscenity." The Supreme Court also stated that there were no articles or clauses in the Constitution that could force individual states to drop controls on commercialized obscenity. Moreover, the Court ruled that Congress has the legal authority to stop the transportation of obscene material on common carriers such as airlines and trucks, and that Congress also has the power to stop any individual or company from importing such materials for private or commercial use.

Film and stage producers as well as publishers admitted that they were confused by the Supreme Court rulings. Although the decisions gave states the power to control or censor pornography, they also gave states the freedom to be permissive. Since the standards set in one community would not necessarily apply to other localities, what might be deemed pornographic in one state could be acceptable in another.

The Supreme Court in Georgia, one of the first states to take action after the United States Supreme Court decisions were handed down, ruled that the motion picture *Carnal Knowledge* was obscene, and, by doing so, upheld a decision made by a lower court in Georgia. This ruling added further confusion to the problem of censorship, particularly for film producers and theater owners because the picture had been rated *R* (children not admitted unless accompanied by an adult) rather than *X* (children not admitted). The Georgia State Supreme Court ruling against *Carnal Knowledge* was appealed and was later overturned by a unanimous decision of the United States Supreme Court.

By the end of the summer of 1973, suits were being prepared in several states to test the constitutionality of obscenity laws. Irwin Karp, the general counsel for the Authors League and the Dramatists

Guild, filed a brief on behalf of these writers' organizations with the United States Supreme Court asking that the court's decision in the *Miller* v. *California* case be reconsidered. Mr. Karp stressed the fact that the "literary, artistic, political, or scientific value of a book" should not be determined by "community standards." He further stated that a book or film which has "serious" literary or artistic value is, under the ruling set by the Supreme Court, still protected by the First Amendment against censorship or banning, even though it may be considered offensive in some states. Karp also stated that he did not believe the United States Supreme Court's sanction of "statewide community standards" gave the same authority to "local communities." If it did, the vast number of small, local communities could create a great jumble of censorship rulings that would lack uniformity and would ban books and films of "substantial literary and artistic value" dealing with sexual themes. Moreover, the Court should clarify its decision by stating that communities could not set their own standards of obscenity but should be required to use the three points of the *Miller* decision specified by the United States Supreme Court. Other attorneys, as well as producers and distributors, agreed with Karp that standards should be set by competent judges. Critics, scholars, and other literary experts, for example, would be better qualified to recognize the "literary value" of a book than jurors or judges who were not experts in the field.

Although theatrical producers realized that the Supreme Court decision could apply to stage plays as well as to films and books, they did not anticipate vice crusaders in New York pressuring for censorship as they had in the 1920s. On the other hand, the producers were concerned about problems that could develop when they sent productions on tour. Censors who had formerly banned plays in Chicago, Philadelphia, Boston, and Los Angeles would now have the authority to ban any play that they considered obscene. Many managers, therefore, predicted that they would either have to be more selective in bookings or else be prepared to edit, cut, or revise productions in cities where nudity would not be permitted or the dialogue might be declared obscene.

Within the next three years, sporadic attempts were made to ban or censor theatrical productions across the country. In the spring of 1974, in Cambridge, Massachusetts, for example, charges of "open and gross lewdness" were made against twelve persons connected with a production of *Sweet Eros* at Theater II in Cambridge. *Sweet Eros* and *Witness,* two one-act plays by Terrence McNally, had been presented off Broadway in New York on November 21, 1968. In *Sweet Eros,* a young man who has tied a girl to a chair rants and sermonizes as he strips the girl and then prepares to rape her. Judge Lawrence F. Feloney in East Cambridge District Court dismissed the charges against ten of the accused. The charges of simulating the sex act on stage made against two of the actors, however, were not dropped. The defense attorney for the actors said that the state laws pertaining to nudity and simulated sex acts did not apply to theatrical productions; therefore the charges made, according to the attorney, violated the First Amendment of the Constitution, which guaranteed freedom of expression.

Variety reported that although performances of *Sweet Eros* were permitted to continue, the two actors still facing charges were not permitted to appear in the nude. The man wore briefs; the girl, panties. Following the court hearing, state and Cambridge police officers, the assistant district attorney of Middlesex County, and a state policeman in plainclothes attended the next performance. The defense attorney later said that police officers were coming to every performance and that the state was paying six dollars a ticket for every officer who checked on the production.

Equus by Peter Shaffer, a drama that included a nude scene and an attempted simulated sex scene, opened in New York on October 24, 1974. It received both the New York Drama Critics Circle and Tony Awards as the best play of the season. John Dexter also received a Tony Award as best director, and Otis L. Guernsey, Jr., selected *Equus* as one of the best plays of the season for his annual volume. The plot dealt with a psychiatrist who tries to help a young man whose love for horses has prevented him from having a normal sexual relationship with a girl. In despair, the young man brutally blinds the horses.

In October, 1976, *Variety* reported that the producers of the touring company were unable to present *Equus* at the State Fair Music Hall in Dallas, Texas, because the theater had already been booked for another attraction. The McFarlin Auditorium at Southern Methodist University was the second choice, but attorneys for the church-affiliated school said the nude scene made the play unacceptable for presentation in the school auditorium. The Memorial Theatre at the Convention Centre also refused to book *Equus* because it would violate a city ordinance, which specified that no scenes with total nudity could be presented in any municipal building that had a liquor license. *Equus,* therefore, was booked into the Will Rogers Auditorium in Fort Worth, Texas. This change in locale was not unprecedented. In 1971, when *Hair* was not permitted to open in Dallas because of its nude scene, the musical was booked into the Will Rogers Auditorium in Fort Worth, which had no law against nudity nor did the theater have a liquor license.

Can New York Solve the Problem?

IN THE LATE 1960s and early 1970s, producers and theater owners in New York felt helpless in their attempts to stop the deterioration of the Broadway theatrical sector. The increasing number of pornographic film houses, massage parlors, "adult" bookstores, hotels that catered to prostitutes and their customers, peep shows, and theaters that presented hard-core stage shows were overrunning Forty-second Street from the Avenue of the Americas (Sixth Avenue) to beyond Eighth Avenue, and Eighth Avenue from Fourteenth Street to Fifty-eighth Street. Some of the side streets in the heart of the theater district were no longer safe at night, and in order to draw ticket buyers, producers were changing schedules and offering four matinees and four evening performances a week instead of the customary six evening performances and two matinees. Actors began reporting that they were being attacked as they left the stage door after an evening's performance. Producers, theater owners, and actors constantly asked for more police protection.

In *Best Plays of 1973–1974,* Otis L. Guernsey, Jr., reported that the Times Square area seemed to be well policed, and that both Mayors Lindsay and Beame had worked almost continuously with Broadway groups and city organizations to prevent further encroachment on the Broadway sector by undesirable elements. Moreover, when an operator tried to take over a Broadway theater and make it a showcase for pornographic films, enough pressure was brought to stop the project after the first day.

Announcements in the summer of 1976 that two productions featuring total nudity, *Let My People Come* and *Oh! Calcutta!,* were booked into two Broadway theaters dismayed the New York League of Theaters and Producers. The board of governors held a special meeting on June 28, 1976, to discuss the booking of *Let My People Come,* and the board drafted a resolution stating that permitting *Let My People Come* to open at the Morosco Theater, one of the more desirable playhouses, was not in keeping with the stand the League had taken against nude shows. At the meeting, however, the League took no formal action.

The operator of the Morosco Theater agreed with the League in objecting to the booking, but he also said he had rented the theater to producer Phil Osterman because he did not want to be considered a censor. Since the Morosco Theater had no current attraction, he had agreed to permit *Let My People Come* to open at the theater but only on an interim booking, since another play, *The Innocents,* was scheduled to open at the Morosco in October. The operator of the Morosco also admitted that he had not seen *Let My People Come* nor did he intend to come to the opening performance.

In explaining their opposition to the booking, officials of the League said they had been exerting pressure on New York City authorities to close such operations as pornographic film houses, "adult" bookstores, peep shows, and massage parlors in the Times Square area. Therefore, they had to stop any sex shows from operating in their own theaters or they would negate all their efforts to clean up the Broadway theatrical section. The League's attempt to prevent *Let My People Come* from opening on Broadway was not the only opposition the production had encountered. The show, written by Earl Wilson, Jr., had opened on January 8, 1974, at the Village Gate Theater in Greenwich Village and, in spite of attempts to evict it, had grossed over $3,500,000 and had run 1,250 performances. *Let My People Come* had never had an official opening date off Broadway nor had the critics been asked to review it. Those who did had paid for their own tickets and had written negative reviews. The show had also been produced in London where it ran almost three years.

Before *Let My People Come* began presenting previews at the Morosco Theater, Earl Wilson, Jr., refused to let his name be used in connection with the production. *Variety* reported that the playbill carried the following insert: "As the author and composer of *Let My People Come,* I am removing my name from credits of this Broadway production because the manner in which my songs have been dramatized is not in keeping with the original interpretation I had intended." Phil Osterman, the producer and director, said he "regretted Wilson's action," but that he, as director, had made revisions that he thought would be better for "the show in the new location." Osterman enlarged the cast from twelve to twenty-two and added five musicians to the orchestra, but he said he had made no changes in the music or lyrics. When *Let My People Come* began giving preview performances at the Morosco, Osterman announced, and then canceled, three official opening dates. Those critics who reviewed the show paid for their tickets and panned the production. *Variety's* reporter, who also bought his tickets at the box office, said his comments were based on just the "mercifully short first act" and closed his review with *"Let My People Come* isn't naughty or shocking—it's just a numbing bore."

The League of New York Theaters and Producers, which had taken no official action against *Let My People Come,* became aroused when Hillard Elkins announced that he was bringing a revival of his erotic revue, *Oh! Calcutta!*, back to Broadway. Elkins had had problems in finding a suitable playhouse, for he had been turned down by theater managers in Chicago as well as in New York. By August, 1976, however, Elkins had made arrangements to present *Oh! Calcutta!* at the Edison Theater (in the Edison Hotel) in a repertory schedule with *Me and Bessie,* a black musical about singer Bessie Smith, which was currently playing at the theater. The two productions would operate on a seven day–thirteen performance schedule. *Me and Bessie* would be given for seven performances on Sunday, Wednesday, Thursday, and Saturday; *Oh! Calcutta!*, for six performances on Sunday, Monday, Tuesday, Friday, and Saturday. Three performances were scheduled for both Saturday and Sunday. Norman Kean, producer of *Me and Bessie* and owner of the Edison Theater, said the repertory program would cut down on overhead, particularly in theater rentals.

To formulate an official policy opposing performances of sex shows on Broadway, the League of New York Theaters and Producers held a special meeting on August 31, 1976, and unanimously passed a resolution that makes the production or presentation of a show that the League considers objectionable sufficient grounds for dismissal from the League. The resolution was based on a clause in the by-laws of the League that specified that such dismissal from membership could be made by a two-thirds vote. The resolution, however, would not affect productions that had already opened or were scheduled to open with a confirmed booking. These shows included *Let My People Come,* which was still presenting previews (and closed October 2, 1976, without having an official opening date), and the revival of *Oh! Calcutta!*, scheduled to begin September 24. Gerald Schoenfeld, a member of the Shubert organization and also a member of the Mayor's Committee on Improvement of Midtown, who had drafted the resolution, also stressed the fact that permitting objectionable productions to play on Broadway counterbalances all efforts of the League to clean up the theatrical sector. The members of the League realized that the resolution in itself, without cooperation and support from government agencies and officials, would not curb the activities of sex peddlers who had increased rather than decreased the number of their establishments.

Hope for an effective clean-up campaign came late in 1976 when Mayor Abraham Beame's administration proposed zoning regulations for New York City to limit the spread of businesses dealing with pornography. These were based, in part, on regulations enacted in the city of Detroit. The legality of such zoning laws was challenged, and in June, 1976, the United States Supreme Court handed down a decision upholding the restrictions set by Denver officials. New Yorkers had anticipated that city officials, in keeping with the Supreme Court's ruling, would take some action. The Department of City Planning and the Mayor's Midtown Action Office not only checked methods to stop the spread of sex theaters, book shops, and similar operations, but also began investigating the possibility of closing many of these questionable establishments now in operation.

In its November 17, 1976, issue, *Variety* reported that the proposed new zoning regulations, if enacted into law, would establish a limit of ten "adult" establishments in the Times Square area. These would include sex-oriented filmhouses, peep shows, book stores, and topless bars. The total of all these establishments in Manhattan would be limited to twenty-eight. Nine of these twenty-eight would be legal between Pennsylvania Station and Bryant Park; five would be located on Lexington Avenue from Fiftieth to Sixtieth Streets; and four would be located east of Third Avenue from Fortieth to Fiftieth Street. *Variety*'s report also stated that New York city officials estimated there were currently 180 "sex-oriented establishments" in Manhattan, and that about 160 were located in the midtown area. The new zoning laws, therefore, would close approximately 150 of these operations. Practically all of the "adult establishments" on Eighth Avenue would be closed. On Forty-second Street, sometimes called "Sin Street," approximately eleven film houses, plus bookstores and peep shows would be cut to a maximum of three.

Operators of "adult" establishments had disregarded earlier attempts to clean up the district. For the first time, however, these operators, faced with the possibility of being put out of business, were prepared to take legal action. The attorney for the operators said the decision of the United States Supreme Court in Denver gave city authorities the right to stop the growth of sex-oriented establishments, but the power to close sites already in operation was still untested in the courts. Therefore, if New York were to enact and then enforce such foreclosures, the operators facing eviction would appeal to higher courts.

Some of the city planners felt that in order to close establishments, the city would have to condemn the property and then buy it from the owners, but such a plan would be impossible for New York in its present economic crisis. Moreover, it is doubtful if the state or national government could or would provide financial aid. Furthermore, the planning commission would have to estimate the cost of so extensive a project before soliciting help.

The League of New York Theaters and Producers, nevertheless, is hopeful that some sort of clean-up campaign will get under way, for any improvement in the theater area, according to League members, would probably bring more theatergoers back into the Broadway sector. The League's resolution to dismiss any member who presented an objectionable production, therefore, would be more effective.

The censorship of stage presentations, regardless of arguments for or against the freedom of expression in art, will ultimately be decided by audiences. Unless dramatic ventures are subsidized, or presented for an extensive list of subscribing members, or presold to a sufficient number of theater party organizations, producers can no longer afford to gamble on plays or musicals that will offend theatergoers. In New York, the rising costs of theater operations and the steady increase in ticket prices, which reached a twenty dollar top for several musicals in 1976, have made theatergoers more selective in choosing an evening out that would cost anywhere from twenty-five dollars to fifty dollars. The box office receipts, therefore, will influence the type of plays produced, for audience reaction will determine whether the theater becomes more permissive or more restrictive.

Selected Bibliography

The author consulted newspaper and magazine articles as well as the printed texts of plays. He also covered extensively references to drama in the *New York Times,* the *London Times, Life, Time,* and *Newsweek.* For news clippings on the American theater before 1900, he used the files of the late Dr. Harold W. Schoenberger. For clippings from 1900 to 1950, he referred to the files of the late Dr. Ralph H. Ware. In addition he checked programs, news items, and clipped criticisms on file in the Curtis Theatre Collection in the University of Pittsburgh Libraries.

American Theatre, The, A Sum of Its Parts. Addresses prepared for a symposium at the first American College Theatre Festival, 1969. New York: Samuel French, 1971.

Archer, William. *The Theatrical World* (4 volumes). London: Walter Scott, 1893, 1894, 1895, 1896.

Baral, Robert. *Revue.* New York: Fleet, 1962.

Best Plays series, edited by G.P. Sherwood and John A. Chapman (1894–1899), Burns Mantle and G.P. Sherwood (1899–1919), Burns Mantle (1919–1920 to 1946–1947), John A. Chapman (1947–1948 to 1951–1952), Louis Kronenberger (1952–1953 to 1959–1960), Henry Hewes (1960–1961 to 1962–1963), Otis L. Guernsey, Jr. (1963–1964 to 1975–1976). New York: Dodd Mead, 1894–1976.

Bunn, Alfred. *The Stage.* London: Bentley, 1840.

Censorship (National Committee against Censorship of the Theatre Arts). American Civil Liberties Union, 1935.

Chandler, Frank W. *Modern Continental Playwrights*. New York: Harper and Brothers, 1931.

Churchill, Allen. *The Great White Way*. New York: Dutton, 1962.

Clark, Barrett H. *Oedipus or Pollyanna*. Seattle: University of Washington Chapbooks, 1928.

Downer, Alan S. *Fifty Years of American Drama, 1900–1950*. Chicago: Regnery, 1951.

Ervine, St. John. *The Theatre in My Time*. London: Rich and Cowan, 1933.

Falk, Bernard. *The Naked Lady*. London: Hutchinson and Co., 1952.

Findlater, Richard. *Banned!* London: MacGibbon and Kee, 1967.

Fowell, Frank and Palmer, Frank. *Censorship in England*. New York: B. Blom, 1969.

Gaver, Jack. *Curtain Calls*. New York: Dodd Mead, 1949.

———. *Season In, Season Out*. New York: Hawthorn, 1966.

Goldman, William. *The Season*. New York: Bantam, 1970.

Gottfried, Morton. *Opening Nights*. New York: Putnam, 1969.

Hibbert, H.G. *Fifty Years of a Londoner's Life*. New York: Dodd Mead, 1916.

Housman, Laurence. *The Unexpected Years*. New York: Bobbs Merrill, 1936.

Hughes, Glenn. *A History of the American Theater, 1700–1950*. New York: Samuel French 1951.

Langner, Lawrence. *The Magic Curtain*. New York: Dutton, 1951.

Mattfeld, Julius. *Variety Music Cavalcade, 1620–1961*. New York: Prentice Hall, 1962.

Morehouse, Ward. *Matinee Tomorrow*. New York: Whittlesey House, 1949.

Moses, Montrose J. and Brown, John Mason. *The American Theater as Seen by Its Critics, 1752–1934*. New York: Norton, 1934.

Nathan, George J. *Encyclopedia of the Theater*. New York: Knopf, 1940.

———. *The Theatre Book of the Year* (from 1942–1943 to 1949–1950). New York: Knopf, 1943–1950.

New York Critics Reviews, New York Critics Reviews, Inc., 1940–.

Nicoll, Allardyce. *History of the English Drama, 1660–1900* (6 volumes). Cambridge: Cambridge University Press, 1952–1960.

Palmer, John. *The Censor and the Theater.* New York: Mitchell Kennerley, 1913.

Pearson, Hesketh. *Oscar Wilde, His Life and Wit.* New York and London: Harper and Brothers, 1946.

Quinn, Arthur Hobson. *A History of the American Drama, Vol. I, From the Beginning to the Civil War.* New York: Appleton-Century-Crofts, 1951.

———. *A History of the American Drama, Vol. II, From the Civil War to the Present.* New York: Appleton-Century-Crofts, 1964.

Shaw, Bernard. *Our Theaters in the Nineties,* Vols. I–III. London: Constable and Co., 1932.

Sherek, Henry. *Not in Front of the Children.* London: Heinemann, 1959.

Skinner, Richard Dana. *Our Changing Theater.* New York: Dial, 1933.

Stagg, Jerry. *The Brothers Shubert.* New York: Random House, 1968.

Taubman, Howard. *The Making of the American Theater.* New York: Coward-McCann, 1965.

Toohey, John L. *The History of the Pulitzer Prize Plays.* New York: The Citadel Press, 1967.

Waldau, Roy S. *1928–1939, The Vintage Years of the Theatre Guild.* Cleveland and London: 1972.

Wilson, Earl. *The Show Business Nobody Knows.* New York: Bantam, 1973.

Index